# Effects of Christianity on Behaviour, Attitudes and Lifestyles

Sheila Butler

Philip Allan Updates, an imprint of Hodder Education, part of Hachette Livre UK, Market Place, Deddington, Oxfordshire OX15 0SE

*Orders*

Bookpoint Ltd, 130 Milton Park, Abingdon, Oxfordshire OX14 4SB

tel: 01235 827720

fax: 01235 400454

e-mail: uk.orders@bookpoint.co.uk

Lines are open 9.00 a.m.–5.00 p.m., Monday to Saturday, with a 24-hour message answering service. You can also order through the Philip Allan Updates website: www.philipallan.co.uk

© Philip Allan Updates 2008

ISBN 978-1-84489-751-3

Impression number   5 4 3 2 1
Year    2012   2011   2010   2009   2008

All rights reserved; no part of this publication may be reproduced, stored in a retrieval system, or transmitted, in any form or by any means, electronic, mechanical, photocopying, recording or otherwise without the either the prior written permission of Philip Allan Updates or a licence permitting restricted copying in the United Kingdom issued by the Copyright Licensing Agency Ltd, Saffron House, 6–10 Kirby Street, London EC1N 8TS.

All photographs are reproduced by permission of TopFoto, with the exception of those otherwise credited.

Design by Neil Fozzard

Printed in Italy.

Hachette Livre UK's policy is to use papers that are natural, renewable and recyclable products and made from wood grown in sustainable forests. The logging and manufacturing processes are expected to conform to the environmental regulations of the country of origin.

# Contents

Introduction .................................................................................. vi

## 1 Ways in which Christians make moral decisions ........................... 1
Sources of morality ........................................................................ 2
Questions and activities ................................................................. 4

## Decisions on life and living

## 2 Sex, marriage and divorce ............................................................ 8
Sexual relationships ....................................................................... 8
Marriage ...................................................................................... 11
Divorce, annulment and remarriage ............................................. 16
Questions and activities ............................................................... 19

## 3 Abortion .................................................................................... 23
The law in the UK ....................................................................... 23
Arguments for and against abortion ............................................. 26
Central issues about abortion ....................................................... 27
Christian attitudes to abortion ..................................................... 29
Questions and activities ............................................................... 31

## 4 Euthanasia ................................................................................. 35
Types of euthanasia ..................................................................... 36
Arguments for and against euthanasia .......................................... 38
Christian attitudes to euthanasia .................................................. 39
Questions and activities ............................................................... 40

## 5 The environment ....................................................................... 43
Environmental problems .............................................................. 43
What can be done? ...................................................................... 45
Christian attitudes to the environment ........................................ 47
Questions and activities ............................................................... 48

## 6 Biblical passages ........................................................................ 52

# Contents

## Justice and reconciliation

### 7 Introduction .................................................. 58
Justice ........................................................... 58
Reconciliation ................................................. 59
Peace ............................................................ 60
Forgiveness .................................................... 60
Questions and activities .................................... 61

### 8 Crime and punishment ................................ 62
Crime and sin ................................................. 62
Why do people commit crime? ......................... 63
Aims of punishment ........................................ 64
Forms of punishment ...................................... 64
Capital punishment ......................................... 67
Christian attitudes to crime and punishment ..... 68
Questions and activities .................................... 71

### 9 War and peace ............................................. 75
Causes of war ................................................. 75
Consequences of war ...................................... 75
Types of weapons and warfare ......................... 77
Terrorism ........................................................ 79
The 'just' war theory ....................................... 80
Pacifism ......................................................... 80
Christian attitudes to war and peace ................. 81
Christian attitudes to protest ............................ 83
Questions and activities .................................... 83

### 10 Biblical passages ......................................... 88

## Christian responsibility

### 11 Prejudice and discrimination ...................... 96
What are prejudice and discrimination? ............ 96
Causes of prejudice and discrimination ............. 96

Effects of Christianity on Behaviour, Attitudes and Lifestyles

Discrimination and the law ............................................. 97
Racial discrimination .................................................... 97
Gender discrimination .................................................. 99
Disability discrimination .............................................. 100
Christian attitudes to prejudice and discrimination ........ 101
Martin Luther King Jr ................................................. 103
Nelson Mandela and Desmond Tutu ............................ 104
Questions and activities .............................................. 106

## 12 World poverty ........................................... 110
The situation ............................................................. 110
The response ............................................................. 114
Christian attitudes to world poverty ............................ 116
Questions and activities .............................................. 117

## 13 Biblical passages ....................................... 121

## Exam technique ............................................ 127

## Glossary ....................................................... 129

## Useful websites ............................................ 134

## Index ........................................................... 135

# Introduction

This book gives you the information and guidance you need to be successful in the AQA GCSE Religious Studies Specification A Option 2A exam, whether Short or Full Course. The title of this module is 'Effects of Christianity on Behaviour, Attitudes and Lifestyles'.

The book covers all areas of the specification, in the same order as the specification. Where appropriate, the set topics are studied from different denominational perspectives.

## The exam

Success in the exam is not just about what you know and understand. It also depends on having the right exam technique. Some questions (usually the shorter ones) require purely factual answers. Others require an ability to apply Christian beliefs to the philosophical and moral issues set for study. There is guidance on exam technique towards the end of this book. You should refer to this throughout your course, particularly when you write answers to essay questions.

## Using this book

This book is divided into sections covering each of the set topics. Each section follows the same format and provides the information you need to tackle any questions you might be set. In the specification, the topics are grouped together under a general heading and have set biblical passages assigned to them. In this book, the topics are separated into different sections. When all the topics under the same specification heading have been covered, there is a section that covers the set biblical passages. You should refer to this as you read each topic. In the exam you may be asked to show detailed knowledge of these passages, as well as an understanding of how they might apply to particular moral issues.

As each topic is investigated, additional biblical passages may be used to explain Christian attitudes. You will not be asked direct questions on these, but you will be given credit for relevant use of them in your answers.

There will also be reference to the beliefs and teachings of different Christian denominations, such as those in the Catechism of the Catholic Church. Again, you will not be asked direct questions on any specific Church statement, but you may receive credit for referring to them. It is essential that you understand a variety of Christian viewpoints and teachings on the set topics, whether or not you agree with them, and that your own views on them are carefully thought out.

At the end of each section on the topics there are various features:

- **Sample questions and answers** These are intended to show you the kind of question you might be asked in an exam and the standard of answer to aim at.
- **Further questions** These are for you to use as exam practice and to help you acquire the right technique.
- **Class activities** These are intended for you to complete individually, in pairs or groups under the direction of your teacher, to add breadth to your knowledge and depth to your understanding.
- **Homework** For some of these tasks you will need access to the internet.
- **Useful websites** These are appropriate to the section topic.

Section 1 is a short introductory section that outlines ways in which Christians approach moral decision-making and the sources of moral authority they might use. Although no questions are set on this in the exam and there are no questions based on it, reading this section and doing the activities will help you with everything that follows.

At the end of the book there are a glossary and a list of websites that are generally relevant for the course. You will find the glossary useful for reference and revision of key words and definitions.

# Section 1
# Ways in which Christians make moral decisions

To a certain extent the approach all humans, Christians included, take to moral decision-making depends on how they see things generally. Some people have fixed ideas — things are either good or bad and right or wrong whatever the circumstances. Their opinions do not change. When it comes to ethics, this approach is known as **absolute morality**. Many people, however, have a more flexible and open approach to life. They may think that something is usually right or wrong, but that in some circumstances rules should be broken and a different decision should be made. This is known as **relative morality**. Others take this even further and think that there is no generally applicable standard on what is right and wrong. Each situation has to be considered separately and independently of rules or previous situations.

### Key words
**Absolute morality**
A type of morality that has fixed and unchanging rules

**Relative morality**
A type of morality which takes the situation and circumstances into account

# Ways in which Christians make moral decisions

## Sources of morality

Sometimes when you are faced with having to make a moral decision, there is no problem. It is clear what you should do. However, at other times you may be faced with a really difficult dilemma. In such situations you might need guidance or advice. You might ask your parents or friends, or you might rely on past experience. There are many sources of possible guidance. Christians might seek guidance and justify their actions from one or more of the following sources.

### The Bible

The Bible, and especially the New Testament, is a sacred text. This means that Christians believe it has special authority and respect its teachings and guidance. It is regarded as the word of God, but Christians understand this in different ways.

> **Key words**
>
> **Christian denominations**
> The different Christian traditions, e.g. Anglican, Roman Catholic
>
> **Fundamentalist Christian**
> Someone who believes that the Bible was inspired directly by God and contains no errors. Its teachings are always relevant
>
> **Liberal Christian**
> Someone who believes that God guided the writers of the Bible, but that there are mistakes and some of its teachings are out of date

Some believe that those who wrote the books contained in the Bible were directly inspired by God, and that the teachings of Jesus and Paul in particular are to be followed absolutely by all Christians at all times. They adopt a **fundamentalist Christian** approach. Others take a more **liberal Christian** approach, believing that the writers were guided by God rather than directly inspired by him. God did not override their human limitations and sometimes they got it wrong. Liberal Christians believe that some of the Bible's teachings, laws and rules are outdated, so they need to be adapted or abandoned altogether.

### Religious leaders

Most **Christian denominations** have leaders who are regarded as experts in understanding and explaining the Bible. For Roman Catholics, the pope is an important source of moral guidance and a role model. The current pope is Benedict XVI.

Effects of Christianity on Behaviour, Attitudes and Lifestyles

Throughout the centuries there have been Christians who have devoted themselves to the service of others and who are sources of inspiration. Notable twentieth-century examples include:

- Mother Teresa
- Martin Luther King Jr (see page 103)
- Maximilian Kolbe
- Nelson Mandela (see page 104)
- Desmond Tutu (see page 104)
- Oscar Romero (see page 68)
- Li Tim-Oi (see page 103)

Pope Benedict XVI

# Ways in which Christians make moral decisions

## Church teaching

This is important for many Christians, especially Roman Catholics. Many documents written or approved by the pope set out central beliefs and teachings that all Roman Catholics are expected to obey. Some deal with specific issues, such as the Vatican Declaration on Euthanasia. Others, such as the **Catechism of the Catholic Church**, cover every aspect of the faith.

> **Key words**
>
> **Catechism of the Catholic Church**
> A book containing the official teaching of the Roman Catholic Church on all matters of faith and practice

Other denominations also produce documents that set out thinking on key issues. For example, in recent decades the Anglican Church has produced reports relating to euthanasia, urban poverty and nuclear weapons.

## Reason

Many Christians believe they should use their minds to think through problems so that they are not swayed by emotions in issues like abortion. This is especially important if the Bible needs to be interpreted or if it does not contain guidance on the issue.

## Conscience

Many Christians think conscience is a moral guide — something that helps them to make the right decisions and that makes them feel guilty if they choose the wrong path. Many also believe it is something that develops as they mature and as a result of their upbringing and education.

# Questions and activities

## Class activities and homework

### Absolute and relative morality

In 2000 Siamese twins, Jodie and Mary, were born in Manchester. If they were left conjoined, they would survive only for a few months. If they were separated, Jodie would probably survive although she would need surgery and might be disabled, but Mary would certainly die. The doctors wanted to separate the twins but the parents opposed it. Three judges were given the task of deciding the outcome. In small groups, find out about this case and read the points made by the doctors and appeal judges. Then discuss the following questions and, under the supervision of your teacher, feed back your answers to the rest of the class. You will find the information you need by using the search engine on http://news.bbc.co.uk.

**a** Why would those who believe in absolute morality argue it was wrong to separate Jodie and Mary?

**b** Why might some who believe in relative morality also argue it was wrong to separate the twins?

**c** Why would most who believe in relative morality support the separation?

**d** What does your group think about this case?

'Parents should have the right to decide for their children. Doctors and lawyers should not interfere.' Do you agree? Give reasons for your answer, showing that you have thought about more than one point of view. Refer to Christian arguments in your answer.

## Sources of moral decision-making

In pairs, take an A3 sheet of paper. Write the title 'Ways in which to make moral decisions'. At the top left-hand corner, write 'Moral problem' and in the bottom right-hand corner, 'Decision made'. Then write on different parts of the page the five most important sources of moral guidance that you would turn to in order of their importance. Write the most important nearest the top left-hand corner and the least important nearest the bottom right-hand corner. Draw a line from the top corner to the bottom, linking up those words with the moral sources you have chosen. Then on the sheet write more sources of moral authority that people turn to, but do not put a line through them. Be prepared to justify your selection to the rest of the class.

Explain how different approaches to the Bible (e.g. fundamentalist, liberal) might affect the way Christians use it when trying to make a moral decision. Give examples in your answer.

## Ways in which Christians make moral decisions

'You should always obey your conscience.' Do you agree? Give reasons for your answer, showing that you have thought about more than one point of view. Refer to Christian arguments in your answer.

## Useful websites

http://news.bbc.co.uk

www.request.org.uk

# Decisions on life and living

# Section 2

# Sex, marriage and divorce

## Sexual relationships

### Changed attitudes to sexual relationships

Matt Lucas and Kevin McGee. Registering a civil partnership allows gay couples to enjoy the same rights as married couples

Attitudes to sexuality and sexual relationships have changed considerably since the middle of the last century. Changes in laws relating to **homosexuality** have meant that gay men and women can 'come out' without fear, although there are still instances of violence against them. Gay couples are now more open about their relationships and can legally register their partnerships in **civil partnership ceremonies**. This gives them rights similar to those of married couples.

### Key words

**Civil partnership ceremonies**
Non-religious ceremonies that allow gay couples to legally register their partnerships

**Homosexuality**
Being sexually attracted to people of the same sex

Effects of Christianity on Behaviour, Attitudes and Lifestyles

Safe **contraception** and abortion mean that unmarried people no longer fear sexual relationships leading to pregnancy. Attitudes to children born outside marriage have also changed and the UK has the highest teenage pregnancy rate in Europe.

The media emphasise sex as something to be enjoyed and tend to assume that people are sexually active at a young age. Many teenage magazines focus on sexual issues, and sex is a prominent theme of many television programmes and films.

## Different types of extra-marital sexual relationships

It is important to distinguish between sex between two single people (often referred to as **pre-marital sex**) and sex where at least one of the two people is married to someone else (**adultery**). With pre-marital sex there is also another distinction that some religious believers make: recreational or **casual sex** (e.g. one-night stands), and sex within a relationship (e.g. two people who live together without being married). Living together without being married is known as **cohabitation**.

## Christian attitudes to sexual relationships

Sexuality is seen as one of God's most precious gifts. Genesis describes Adam's delight when Eve was created and the joy of their sexual relationship:

> The man and the woman were both naked, and they felt no shame.
>
> (Genesis 2:25)

The Song of Solomon, also in the Old Testament, is a collection of explicit love poems.

> How beautiful your sandaled feet,
> O prince's daughter!
> Your graceful legs are like jewels,
> the work of a craftsman's hands.
>
> (Song of Solomon 7:1)

### Key words

**Adultery**
A sexual relationship between two people, at least one of whom is married to someone else

**Casual sex**
Sex without commitment

**Cohabitation**
A couple living together and enjoying a sexual relationship without being married

**Contraception**
A range of methods that may be used to prevent pregnancy

**Extra-marital sex**
A sexual relationship between two people who are not married to each other. They may be single or married to someone else

**Pre-marital sex**
Sexual intercourse prior to marriage

## Decisions on life and living — Sex, marriage and divorce

After his conversion to Christianity, Paul travelled through countries in Europe, telling anyone who would listen about Jesus. He made many converts and kept in touch with them, answering questions and giving moral and spiritual guidance in letters. In most of his letters he discussed sexual relationships, but this was a particular issue for the church community at Corinth. They asked him whether or not they should marry and his reply displayed a far more cautious attitude to sexual relationships than is seen in the Old Testament. This was partly because he saw clearly from the pagan environment in which he lived that uncontrolled sexuality could have terrible results. The Corinthians were notoriously promiscuous. He also believed that the end of the world was imminent, so Christians should be preparing for that instead of being distracted by sex. He told the Christians at Corinth to remain celibate but if their sexual urges were strong they should marry, for there was no shame in it. He also told them that their bodies were temples of the Holy Spirit. They should respect their bodies as they would a place of worship (1 Corinthians 6:18–20).

### Key words

**Celibacy**
Not having a sexual relationship within or outside marriage, often as a result of a religious promise

**Chastity**
Having moral standards and restraint with regard to sexual relations

Throughout the history of the Church, **celibacy** has been valued. Roman Catholic priests are not able to marry and neither are monks and nuns (both Roman Catholic and Anglican). Some Christians choose celibacy as a way of showing their devotion to God.

For most Christians, however, sexual relationships are important. The official teaching of all denominations is that sex should be restricted to marriage. This is because marriage demands the commitment needed for the greatest enjoyment of sexual relationships. Marriage also provides a stable environment for rearing children, which the Roman Catholic Church claims is the primary purpose of sex. Christians in other denominations do not agree with this. They think that sexual pleasure is important in its own right, although they would probably agree that the best context for sex is marriage.

A movement to win teenagers back to traditional sexual values and promote **chastity** started in the USA in 1993. It was known as 'True Love Waits'. Teenagers, who may or may not be virgins, promise not to have sex before marriage, and they sign a card. Parents or supporters give the young person a ring, saying, 'Let this ring be a constant reminder to you to be sexually pure.' The 'Silver Ring Thing' movement has now become global.

However, many Christians recognise that society has changed and that the reasons given in the past for confining sex to marriage are no longer valid. These Christians accept loving and committed sexual relationships but do not approve of recreational or casual sex.

Lydia Playfoot took her school to the High Court after she was banned from wearing her silver chastity ring to school

All Christians take seriously the seventh commandment: 'Do not commit adultery' and Jesus's teaching in Matthew 5:27–28 that the thinking and the desire behind adultery is as bad as the act itself. Adultery causes terrible hurt and a sense of betrayal. It is seen as a form of cheating and dishonesty. Once one partner has been unfaithful to the other, it is hard to build up trust again.

## Marriage

Marriage has changed dramatically in the last 30 years. The number of marriages registered each year has halved, and far fewer are religious ceremonies. The average age for marriage has gone up to approximately 30, and increasing numbers are second or third marriages.

# Decisions on life and living — Sex, marriage and divorce

'True Love Waits' challenges teenagers to make a commitment not to have sex until they are married

Marriage is a public declaration of commitment made by one person to another. People get married for all kinds of reasons. They want to share their lives with the one they love. They see marriage as the best way of developing companionship and of giving children a secure environment that will enable them to grow into well-adjusted adults. Some also think that it is the best environment for expressing sexuality.

Marriage is also a legal contract that gives each partner rights. A marriage is not valid unless it has been conducted by a legally authorised individual. This means that sometimes couples have two ceremonies, one civil and one religious.

## Christian attitudes to marriage

Most Christians see marriage as a **sacramental covenant** between two people that has been established by God. Jesus saw marriage as a lifelong commitment. Quoting Genesis, he said:

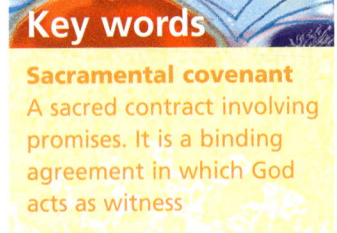

**Key words**

**Sacramental covenant**
A sacred contract involving promises. It is a binding agreement in which God acts as witness

At the beginning of creation God 'made them male and female. For this reason a man will leave his father and mother and be united to his wife, and the two will become one flesh.' So they are no longer two, but one. Therefore what God has joined together, let man not separate.

(Mark 10:6–9)

Effects of Christianity on Behaviour, Attitudes and Lifestyles

In his letter to the Christians of Ephesus, Paul quoted the same Genesis passage. Self-giving love and respect were, he said, the central features of a marriage. He said that the relationship between husband and wife mirrored that between Christ and his Church. The man should love his wife as Christ self-sacrificially loved the Church. More controversially from a modern viewpoint, he said that wives were to submit to their husbands (5:22). Many Christians think that this attitude is out of date. Some fundamentalist Christians, however, believe that wives should obey their husbands, though they point out that Paul's teaching on the kind of love a man should show his wife would prevent him from behaving like a tyrant.

Christian marriages are not arranged, except where particular cultural influences are strong, and there are no racial or religious bans. Christians are expected to ensure that where cultures and/or faiths are different, there is mutual respect and tolerance. Roman Catholics especially are concerned about marriages where one partner is non-Catholic or non-Christian, and a priest would talk this situation over carefully with the couple.

Most Christians also want their parents to approve, as family support is seen as a key factor in the success of a marriage.

Wedding preparation classes are organised by most Christian denominations to ensure that the couple are fully prepared for the difficulties that can occur during the marriage.

Most Christian marriage services follow a similar format. The Anglican ceremony states that marriage:
- was given by God at creation
- entails a process of growth that leads to physical, emotional and spiritual unity and companionship
- is intended to be lifelong
- enables the couple to experience the joy of sexual fulfilment and commitment
- provides a secure environment for bringing up children
- enriches and strengthens society

**Decisions on life and living** — **Sex, marriage and divorce**

In the vows, each partner states the intention of remaining faithful until death, whatever the circumstances:

> for better, for worse,
> for richer, for poorer,
> in sickness and in health,
> to love and to cherish,
> till death us do part.
>
> *(Common Worship Services and Prayers for the Church of England: Marriage © The Archbishop's Council, 2000)*

These vows are made in God's presence and with him as witness. Rings, symbolising unending love and fidelity, are exchanged with the words:

> With my body I honour you, all that I am I give to you, and all that I have I share with you.
>
> *(Common Worship Services and Prayers for the Church of England: Marriage © The Archbishop's Council, 2000)*

A wedding ring is a complete circle with no beginning or end, symbolising eternity

Effects of Christianity on Behaviour, Attitudes and Lifestyles

At this point the priest declares that the two are married and joins together their right hands, quoting Jesus's command not to separate what has been joined by God. The couple are then blessed. The ceremony includes readings and prayers, and often hymns and a short sermon. In Roman Catholic and Anglican churches, Christians often have a **Nuptial Mass**.

The Roman Catholic ceremony also includes the statement that each partner is open to the gift of children, as a blessing from God. This ties in with the view that every sexual act should be both **unitive** and **procreative**.

> **Key words**
>
> **Nuptial Mass**
> A service of Holy Communion held as part of the marriage ceremony
>
> **Procreative sex**
> Sex which has the possibility of conception
>
> **Secular**
> Not religious
>
> **Unitive sex**
> The idea that sexual intercourse makes a couple one

Because of the belief that every act of sexual intercourse should be procreative, Roman Catholic teaching states that artificial forms of contraception (e.g. condoms or the pill) are sinful. In practice, however, some Roman Catholic couples believe that it is a matter for individual conscience and ignore the ruling of the Church. Anglican and other Protestant Christians think that because God intended humans to make some decisions for themselves, using contraception may be a responsible thing to do.

Christians see marriage as a partnership of equals that has to be worked at if it is to succeed. Honesty, respect, commitment, faithfulness and loyalty are essential.

## Why marriages fail

Almost all marriages go through rough patches. This is part of human nature. When major problems occur, **secular** and religious charities or groups may provide support to try to save the marriage or to prevent the break-up from being hostile. For Christians, prayer and reflection on relevant Bible passages are important.

# Decisions on life and living — Sex, marriage and divorce

**Figure 2.1** Why marriage fails

*[Mind map diagram showing "Why marriage fails" at the centre with the following branches and sub-branches:]*

- **Work**
  - Long hours away from home
  - Wife earns more
  - Career comes first
  - Husband not ambitious
- **Infidelity**
  - Loss of trust
  - Hurt
  - Sense of betrayal
- **Money**
  - Debt
  - Job loss
  - Gambling
- **Addiction**
  - Alcohol
  - Drugs
- **Unreasonable behaviour**
  - Physical/mental cruelty
  - Constant nagging
- **Immaturity**
  - Boredom
  - False expectations
  - Married too young
- **Changed circumstances**
  - Long-term sickness
  - Disability
  - Infertility
- **Children**
  - Difficult children
  - One wants them and the other doesn't
  - Children from previous relationships

# Divorce, annulment and remarriage

## The law

Divorce has been transformed over the past 50 years and it is now much easier to obtain one. Divorce is possible after a year of marriage, and one in three marriages ends this way. The sole ground for divorce in the UK is irretrievable breakdown of marriage. Remarriage is allowed without limit.

Effects of Christianity on Behaviour, Attitudes and Lifestyles

If it can be shown that the marriage was never valid in the first place, then it is annulled and there is no need for any divorce procedure. The partners are free to 'remarry'.

## Christian attitudes to divorce and remarriage

All Christians agree that marriage is intended to be lifelong, but there are differences of opinion about divorce and remarriage, partly because marriage is seen as a sacrament by Roman Catholics and some Anglicans, and partly because of differing approaches to the teaching of Jesus and Paul on divorce and remarriage.

According to Mark 10:2–12, Jesus said that divorce was never part of God's purpose. It was a concession to human weakness, and marriage was intended to be for life. Remarriage after divorce was effectively adultery (unless infidelity had been involved, according to Matthew 5:32). This passage from Mark raises a number of questions:

- Was Jesus making a law or stating an ideal?
- Was he trying to protect the status of women, who were made vulnerable by the divorce laws of his day?
- Were some/all of the verses on remarriage after divorce an addition by Mark for the Church in Rome, as women may not divorce men under Jewish law?
- Was the exception for infidelity in Matthew 5:32 an addition made to meet the needs of the Jewish Christian community for which that Gospel was written?

Paul said that couples should not divorce, save where a pagan partner wanted to divorce a husband or wife who had converted to Christianity. In that case, the Christian should agree to the divorce, but only for the sake of peace.

## Roman Catholics

Marriage is a **sacrament**. The vows cannot be dissolved because they are made in the name of God. Jesus was laying down a law for Christians to follow. The Roman Catholic Church does not recognise civil divorce: couples are married for life. Many priests will not allow those who remarry after

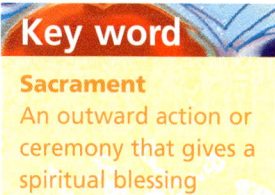

**Key word**

**Sacrament**
An outward action or ceremony that gives a spiritual blessing

**Decisions on life and living** | **Sex, marriage and divorce**

### Key words

**Annulment**
The declaration that a valid marriage never existed

**Eucharist**
One of the Christian sacraments, a service at which Christians eat bread and drink wine in remembrance of Jesus's death

**Reconciliation**
One of the Christian sacraments. It involves confessing your sins to a priest and the priest declaring God's forgiveness

divorce to receive Holy Communion. Those with marital problems should seek help from their families and friends, a marriage counsellor or priest. They should also seek help from the Bible, prayer and the sacraments, especially the **Eucharist** and **Reconciliation**.

A marriage can be ended by an **annulment** if it can be shown never to have been a true marriage. The partners are free to 'remarry'. Grounds for an annulment are if one of the partners:

- was forced into the marriage
- suffered from mental problems at the time
- did not intend to keep the vows
- was not baptised at the time of marriage

## Most Protestant denominations (e.g. Methodists and Baptists)

Although they take the marriage vows seriously, Protestants believe that:

- Humans are not perfect and sometimes divorce is necessary or the best course of action to take.
- Jesus was always willing to forgive and offer people a fresh start.
- Jesus's teaching on marriage was an ideal rather than a law.

Remarriage in church is permissible providing that the vows are taken seriously.

## Anglicans

Marriage is a sacrament and vows made in the presence of God are meant to be kept. An official statement acknowledges that there are situations when divorce and remarriage in church are acceptable, but in practice attitudes vary from church to church.

Some priests adopt the Roman Catholic view and do not see divorce as valid. Others believe that divorce is sometimes the best option. However, since in their view marriage vows can be made only once, they do not allow remarriage in church. Instead, they may hold a service of marriage blessing after a civil ceremony. When Prince Charles married Camilla Parker-Bowles in 2005, they had a civil ceremony at the Guildhall in Windsor, followed by a service of marriage blessing in St George's Chapel, Windsor Castle.

Some priests accept divorce, recognising that people make mistakes. They point to the example of Jesus, who was always willing to give people a second chance. They think that Jesus's teaching about divorce and remarriage was an ideal rather than a rule and accept that second marriages can be better than the first. They are willing to let couples remarry in church providing they take the vows seriously.

Both Prince Charles and Camilla Parker-Bowles had been married before

# Questions and activities

## Sample questions and answers

**1** What is meant by a civil marriage ceremony?  (1 mark)

 It is a non-religious wedding ceremony.

### Commentary

This is only worth 1 mark, so a short answer is sufficient.

**2** Explain the meaning and purpose of marriage for Christians.  (5 marks)

 Many Christians see marriage as a sacrament. This means it is a ceremony that carries God's special blessing. The bride and groom make a covenant with one another in the presence of God and the Church community. They make vows that they will stay together

# Decisions on life and living — Sex, marriage and divorce

for life through thick and thin, and that they will cherish one another. There are three important purposes that marriage fulfils. The man and woman are companions, sharing good and bad experiences together. Their sexual lives are enriched through lovemaking, which is carried out only with each other. They work together to make their home a stable, secure and loving environment in which to bring up children. At the heart of their marriage is mutual love and respect for each other. The everlasting nature of their love is symbolised in the marriage service with the exchange of rings.

## Commentary

The allocation of 5 marks means that a detailed answer is required. This sample answer explains both the meaning of marriage and its purposes, as set out in the Anglican marriage service, and a number of developed points are made.

**3** 'Marriage is totally pointless in our modern world.' Do you agree? Give reasons for your answer, showing that you have thought about more than one point of view. You should refer to Christian teaching in your answer. (5 marks)

So many marriages break up nowadays that marriage does not seem to have any real point. The vows people make seem meaningless. Because people live longer now, the old idea of a lifelong loving relationship just isn't realistic. People change, situations change, and so it is hard for the love to last. Few people have any religious commitments now, so the whole idea of marriage as blessed by God and of making sacred promises is alien. In the past, people were shocked if you lived together and children born out of marriage were looked down on. All that has changed, so it really doesn't matter whether or not you are married.

On the other hand, many couples still choose to marry one another. Living together is just not the same. You don't make a public commitment when you move in with someone. You just move in! It's far too easy to leave if you are cohabiting. If they are married, people might think twice before getting divorced. This means that their children have a better chance of a stable home with two parents. A secure childhood means a secure adult. Although most people today are not practising Christians, they may want to promise to be faithful until death and to share everything. They want God's blessing as they start out on a new life together.

Effects of Christianity on Behaviour, Attitudes and Lifestyles

Overall, I think there is a point to marriage. Many people want to marry. They want it to last and if they have the support of their family and friends, the likelihood is that it will. Yes, one in three marriages breaks down. That means that two in three don't!

## Commentary

It would be easy to answer a question like this without any reference to religious views, but this is a religious studies exam so they must be included. You do not have to give only religious views, nor do you have to be a Christian yourself. You simply have to show how religious beliefs and teachings could support a particular view. You may wish to comment on the strengths or weaknesses of the religious arguments, and this would certainly help you towards gaining full marks. It does not matter whether the examiner agrees with you or not. All the examiner is looking for is your ability to evaluate two points of view and to see how Christian teachings might be relevant.

This answer gives both viewpoints in some detail and ends with a brief conclusion that takes further the argument in support of marriage.

## Further questions

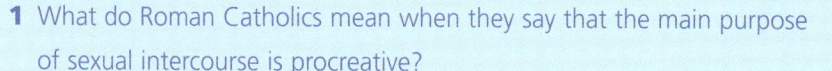

1. What do Roman Catholics mean when they say that the main purpose of sexual intercourse is procreative? (1 mark)
2. Explain some reasons why marriages fail. (3 marks)
3. Do you think couples should stay together for the sake of their children? Give reasons for your answer. (4 marks)
4. 'Couples who have made promises to God and then broken them should not be allowed to remarry in a church.' Give reasons for your answer, showing that you have thought about more than one point of view. Refer to Christian teachings in your answer. (5 marks)

## Class activities and homework

### Finding out from the experts

Your teacher will invite a number of adults into the classroom, who will be prepared to answer questions relating to sex, marriage and divorce. One is likely to be the local priest/vicar. It may be possible to invite a marriage counsellor or legal expert. Bring your questions to the lesson.

# Decisions on life and living — Sex, marriage and divorce

## 'True love waits'

Or does it? In small groups, find out more about the 'True Love Waits' and 'Silver Ring Thing' organisations from the internet and discuss what you think about their views and the way they work. Report back to the rest of the class.

Find out what is involved in getting a divorce from one of the websites that deals with this. Then write an answer to the following: 'Divorce is far too easy. Couples should have to work harder at making their marriages work.' Do you agree? Give reasons for your answer, showing that you have thought about more than one point of view. Refer to Christian teachings in your answer.

## Ten commandments for marriage

Draw up a list of your own ten commandments for marriage. Put them up on display and discuss in groups which commandments you think are the most important.

Choose any television soap and watch five episodes. Study the relationships between couples and note how they develop. Do you think their relationships could be improved and, if so, how? Do you think there is a future for them? Are the couples honest with one another? Do they love each other or are their relationships built on lust or exploitation?

Do you think contraception should be automatically and more easily available to those under the age of 16? Give reasons for your opinion.

## Useful websites

www.request.org.uk  Click on *issues* for Christian views on sex, marriage and divorce.
http://re-xs.ucsm.ac.uk  Click on *World Religions*, then on *Rites of Passage* for information on Christian marriage.
www.silverringthing.org.uk
www.carismag.co.uk

22  Effects of Christianity on Behaviour, Attitudes and Lifestyles

# Section 3

# Abortion

**Abortion** arouses strong emotions. It is easy to get swept away on either side of the debate, but that is to trivialise it. There are serious and strong arguments on both sides that you need to think about rationally. At the same time, you might like to consider whether your view might change if you were personally involved, as a potential parent, relative or friend.

## The law in the UK

The 1967 Abortion Act was passed to stop dangerous 'back-street' abortions. This Act permitted abortion in certain situations. In 1990 some amendments and additions were made.

The law works on the principle of **viability**, so there is a cut-off time of 24 weeks for most abortions. The law currently stands as shown in Figure 3.1 overleaf.

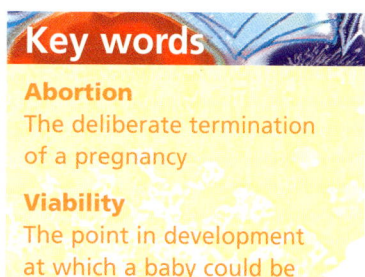

**Key words**

**Abortion**
The deliberate termination of a pregnancy

**Viability**
The point in development at which a baby could be born with some chance of independent survival

GCSE Religious Studies AQA (A) Option 2A

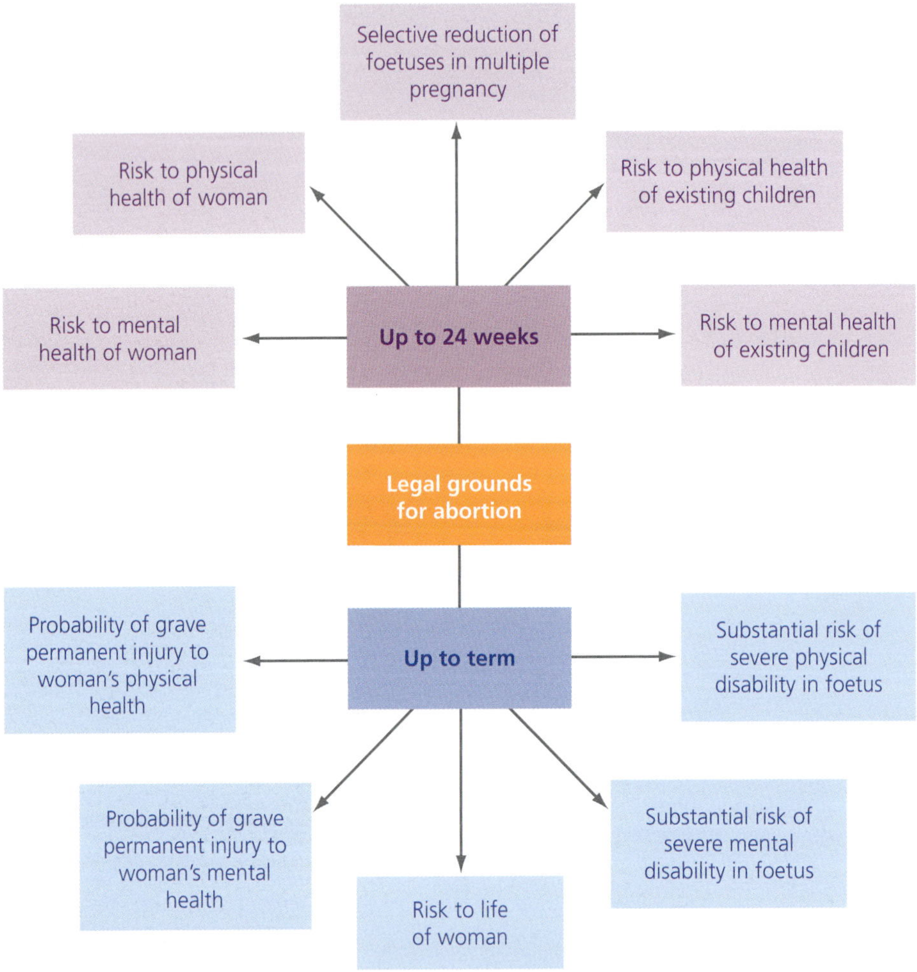

# Decisions on life and living

## Abortion

**Figure 3.1** The legal grounds for abortion

In practice, most abortions are carried out at a fairly early stage on the grounds of risk to the woman's mental health. Foetal rights are protected by the time limits contained in the Abortion Act. The rights of the mother and any existing children are also taken seriously. Doctors and nurses who are totally opposed to abortion do not have to carry out or assist in abortions. However, they must give post-abortion care. Doctors who are unwilling to sign a form allowing an abortion have to pass on their patients to doctors who have no such concerns. The law does not give any rights to potential fathers or personnel involved in the abortion process, such as medical secretaries.

Effects of Christianity on Behaviour, Attitudes and Lifestyles

## Reactions to the law

In recent years there have been calls to tighten up the procedure to prevent 'abortion on demand'. Some people want the 24-week limit reduced.

Abortions are permitted later than 24 weeks if:
- the mother's life is at risk
- there is a risk of grave permanent injury to the mental or physical health of the mother
- there is a substantial risk that if the baby were born it would be severely disabled

However, many doctors are reluctant to perform abortions after 12 weeks. This is partly because by that stage everything is 'in place' — the rest of the pregnancy is largely a matter of growth and maturity of organs. Another reason is that the abortion procedure becomes more complex and distasteful beyond this point. Even more doctors are unhappy about performing abortions in the final **trimester**, especially if the grounds are disability.

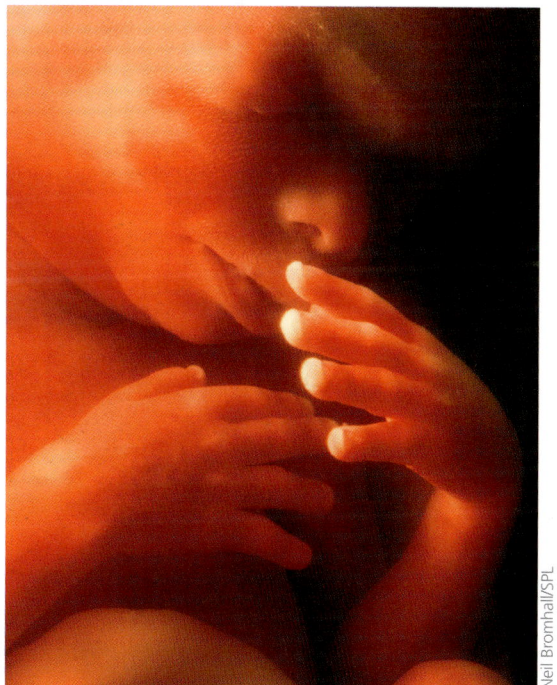

A 5-month old foetus in the womb

**Key word**

**Trimester**
A period of 3 months. Pregnancy may be divided into three trimesters

In 2002, the late abortion of a foetus with a cleft palate led to a court case. There were strong opinions on either side.

In contrast, some groups campaign for abortion on demand at any stage of pregnancy. They argue that the foetus has no rights until it is born, and that the woman is the best person to make a judgement. She has to carry and give birth to the baby. Feminists point out that the law was created by men. Why should they dictate what a woman may do in this most personal of situations?

**Decisions on life and living** — **Abortion**

Rev Joanna Jepson took a health authority to court for allowing the late abortion of a foetus with a cleft lip and palate

## Arguments for and against abortion

Those who support abortion may offer the following reasons:
- The foetus is just a clump of cells or at best only a potential life.
- It is cruel to make a woman go through childbirth if she does not want the child.
- A teenage girl is not ready for the responsibilities of motherhood.
- A woman who has been raped should not have to cope with the product of rape growing and moving inside her.
- The abortion of a disabled foetus is in the best interests of everyone.
- No baby should be born into poverty, and it could make things even worse for the parents and any siblings.
- No child should be unwanted.
- Women have the right to dictate what happens to their bodies and they are the best ones to make an informed decision.

Effects of Christianity on Behaviour, Attitudes and Lifestyles

Those who oppose abortion may offer the following reasons:
- Life begins at conception so the embryo should have equal rights with the mother from the start. It deserves special protection because it is defenceless and vulnerable.
- Effective methods of contraception are available.
- Abortion may lead to terrible feelings of guilt.
- Abortion can cause long-term medical problems.
- It is wrong to punish a child conceived out of rape for the sin of its father.
- Disabled people are capable of fulfilled and happy lives, and support is available.
- Financial, material, emotional and spiritual support is available to mother and child.
- No child need be an unwanted child, but can be adopted.
- The right to **autonomy** is not absolute, especially when it involves harming another being. The woman's emotional involvement may prevent her making the wisest decision.

## Central issues about abortion

There are a number of issues at the heart of the abortion debate:
- Whose rights are the most important?
- When does life begin?
- Which matters most — sanctity of life or quality of life?

### Whose rights are the most important?

**Pro-life** campaigners claim that **foetal rights** need absolute protection because a foetus is unable to defend itself. **Pro-choice** campaigners argue that **maternal rights** should come first. The mother is alive in a way that the foetus is not, and she alone has the right to make decisions about what happens in and to her body.

> **Key words**
>
> **Autonomy**
> The right to make decisions for yourself
>
> **Foetal rights**
> The rights of the unborn child
>
> **Maternal rights**
> The rights of the mother
>
> **Pro-choice**
> Supporting the right of women to decide for themselves whether or not to have an abortion
>
> **Pro-life**
> The anti-abortion view that the foetus has absolute right to life

## Decisions on life and living | Abortion

Pro-life campaigners want to protect foetal rights

### When does life begin?

This issue is relevant for two reasons. First, being alive gives rights. Second, the deliberate killing of a living human is unlawful. To a certain extent, it depends on what you mean by 'life'. If you mean independent life, then it begins at birth because until then the foetus is entirely dependent on the woman carrying it. However, a baby is totally dependent on others, and so is a young child. A baby would not survive for long if it had to fend for itself.

### Key word

**Ensoulment**
The point at which the foetus receives its soul from God, and therefore becomes a person

Many people believe that life begins at conception, when something unique comes into being. Those who take this view speak of **ensoulment** or of the embryo being a human being. Others would say that the embryo is a *potential* person, so has some rights from the start but that full rights are aquired as it develops. Many people see the development of the nervous system and brain activity as particularly significant.

28 Effects of Christianity on Behaviour, Attitudes and Lifestyles

## Is sanctity of life more important than quality of life?

**Sanctity of life** means that life is sacred. It is special, precious and unique. Christians see life as God-given, and so it must be protected and respected. The term applies to both foetus and mother.

**Quality of life** refers to the kind of future the foetus will have. Will it be able to fulfil its potential? Is it wanted? Will it be loved? Will a severely disabled child lead a life full of suffering and frustration? The idea of quality of life is also applied to the mother, especially if she is young.

# Christian attitudes to abortion

Although all Christians believe in the sanctity of life and take the issue of abortion seriously, there are differences of approach. Official Roman Catholic teaching absolutely opposes abortion, whereas many Protestants take a more relativist approach. There are, however, individual Roman Catholics who see abortion as justified in certain situations, and some Protestants who have a more absolutist approach.

## Roman Catholics

Abortion is much the same as murder: a grave sin meriting excommunication. Whether or not the embryo is fully a person at conception, it is entitled to full rights in view of the person it will become. From conception a human being is unique and infinitely precious in God's eyes. The Catechism of the Catholic Church and other Biblical texts support this view:

> My frame was not hidden from you
> when I was made in the secret place.
> When I was woven together in the depths of the earth,
> your eyes saw my unformed body.
> All the days ordained for me
> were written in your book
> before one of them came to be.
>
> (Psalm 139:15–16)

**Key words**

**Quality of life**
Whether or not a person will have a life that is worthwhile and of value

**Sanctity of life**
The idea that life is holy and precious

## Decisions on life and living — Abortion

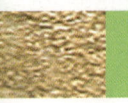

Paralympic athlete Lucia Sosa from Mexico. Roman Catholics believe that God has a plan for every human life

Early Christian writings also support this anti-abortion stance. For example, the Didache (an early-second-century text) prohibits the killing of an unborn child.

The Catechism of the Catholic Church states: 'Human life must be respected and protected absolutely from the moment of conception' and that 'direct abortion… is gravely contrary to the moral law'.

By 'direct abortion', Roman Catholics mean actions intended to kill the foetus. However, they accept that some actions may be necessary to save the mother's life that result in the loss of the foetus. Roman Catholics oppose abortion on the grounds of severe disability, believing that every life is of equal value and has potential and that it is not for humans to pass judgement on quality of life. They also state that it is unfair to punish the foetus for its father's sin in the case of rape, and that the birth of a child in such circumstances represents something good coming out of evil. The child can be adopted or its mother given the support of the Christian community to enable her to give the child a loving upbringing. The Roman Catholic Church has many organisations, both local and national, that provide financial and emotional support for a mother, however young, to cope with pregnancy and looking after the baby.

## Anglicans

The Church of England agrees with the Roman Catholic Church that abortion is morally wrong and is concerned about the number of abortions being performed. Nevertheless, in some circumstances compassion is central to the issue. Anglicans accept abortion to save maternal life and many see it as justified in situations like rape. The official line on disability is that abortions after 24 weeks should only take place where the child would die soon after birth. Most Anglicans accept other types of severe disability as grounds for abortion up to 24 weeks if the mother feels it to be in the child's best interests. Above all, abortion is a matter of individual conscience.

## Methodists

Methodists see abortion as undesirable but believe that it is justified in cases of risk to the life or health of the mother and the existing family, and in cases of great poverty, rape and severe disability.

# Questions and activities

## Sample questions and answers

**1** What is an abortion? (1 mark)

The deliberate termination of a pregnancy.

### Commentary

A short but clear definition is needed. There are other possible answers, e.g. the deliberate killing of a foetus. What matters is that you show the examiner that you know what the term means.

# Decisions on life and living — Abortion

**2** Explain why some Christians think abortion is always wrong.
(4 marks)

Christians believe that life is God-given and sacred, and some think this applies right from when the baby is conceived. To have an abortion is both a rejection of God's gift and an act of unlawful killing. The sixth commandment states 'Do not kill.' The foetus is especially vulnerable and defenceless, and has the right to protection. Some people would claim that to abort a disabled foetus would be an act of compassion, but many Christians would argue that humans do not have the right to make judgements on quality of life and that everyone is equally precious in the eyes of God. It is more compassionate to allow a disabled foetus as full a life as possible than to allow it no life at all.

## Commentary

This question is worth 4 marks and requires detailed discussion of a few points. A basic list giving four simple reasons would not receive more than 2 marks.

**3** 'The abortion of disabled babies should never be allowed.' Do you agree? Give reasons for your answer, showing that you have thought about more than one point of view. Refer to Christian arguments in your answer.
(5 marks)

Some people think it would be terrible for a mother to see her child grow up without fully developed limbs or with the mental age of a toddler. They think that, out of compassion for her, a foetus that is likely to suffer from disabilities should be aborted. They also think that such a child might suffer a lifetime of bullying and also of frustration at not being able to do the same things as its siblings and peers. Jesus said that one of the greatest commandments was to 'love your neighbour as yourself', and the New Testament stresses the importance of showing pity. Any pain suffered by the foetus would be short and preferable to what it would have to put up with if it were born.

I can see that such arguments do make some important points. For religious believers, compassion and love are essential qualities. Nobody likes to see a child suffer. Nevertheless, I do not agree with that view. I do not have any strong religious beliefs myself, but I think that at conception something totally unique comes into being with

Effects of Christianity on Behaviour, Attitudes and Lifestyles

its own genetic structure. Life is sacred. Who are we to judge whether or not a disabled person can lead a worthwhile life? All he or she needs is love, respect and encouragement, which is what all humans need. Loving your neighbour and showing compassion mean enabling people to live to the full, not killing them before they have had the chance. If you watch the Paralympics, you can see that disabled people are no different from those without disability. They enjoy life just as much. Even if the baby's life is short, I think he or she should still have the chance. It is not cruel to the parents. It gives them the opportunity to love the being they have created, to say a proper farewell and to grieve. Many religious believers claim that only God has the right to say when life should end. I think it should end naturally, and not be given a helping hand.

## Commentary

This answer shows a different type of construction from the evaluative response on page 20 in the previous section, where there was a paragraph on each side of the argument followed by a conclusion. Here, the way in which the answer is written means that there is no need for a conclusion. Nevertheless, as it considers two viewpoints, contains religious content and is coherent, it fulfils the criteria for Level 5, which means full marks.

## Further questions

1 Give two situations when the law would allow abortion. (2 marks)
2 Explain why most Christians accept abortion if the woman's life is at risk. (3 marks)
3 Do you think it is acceptable to use abortion as a form of contraception? Give reasons for your answer. (4 marks)
4 Explain different ideas about when the foetus has rights. (4 marks)

## Class activities and homework

### Joanna Jepson and the case of the cleft palate abortion

In pairs, type *Joanna Jepson* into Google and in the search box in the BBC News website at http://news.bbc.co.uk. Find out all you can about the case, and write some questions to put to an 'Any Questions' panel. The panel will consist of a chairperson, Joanna Jepson, a doctor, a representative from LIFE (an anti-abortion group) and a representative from Abortion Rights (which supports abortion on demand).

# Decisions on life and living — Abortion

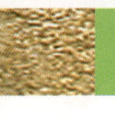

Your teacher will choose five members of your class to take the roles of each of these people. They should research the case and work out what each person might have thought about it. Then hold an 'Any Questions' session.

Create a chart showing the different stages of foetal development. Using different colours and a colour key, mark the point (if you think there is one) at which the foetus is definitely a person, the point at which it is definitely not a person (again, if you think there is one) and the point at which you think the foetus is a person and should have rights.

## Pro-life/pro-choice magazine article

In pairs, create a magazine article of between 100 and 200 words, giving a pro-life or pro-choice view on abortion. You may structure and set out your article as you wish.

Find out and make detailed notes on different Christian viewpoints on abortion. Copy any relevant quotations and highlight the phrases that you would find it useful to learn. Underneath each quote, make a note of whether you would use it in support of or against abortion.

Use the information in this book and the notes you made for yourself to write two paragraphs explaining how Christian beliefs and teachings might affect a religious believer's attitude to abortion.

## Useful websites

www.abortionrights.org.uk

www.bbc.co.uk/religion/ethics  Click on *Abortion*.

http://news.bbc.co.uk

www.prolife.org.uk

www.request.org.uk  Click on *issues*.

http://re-xs.ucsm.ac.uk  Click on *Ethical & Moral Issues*, then on *Abortion*.

www.spuc.org.uk  Click on *Ethical issues*, then on *Abortion*.

www.lifeuk.org  Click on *Education*.

# Section 4

# Euthanasia

**Euthanasia** is an emotive topic. The word literally means 'good death' and is often explained as 'mercy killing' or 'dying with dignity'.

Although euthanasia is legal in some countries such as the Netherlands, in the UK it is illegal. Those involved are at best charged with assisting suicide and at worst with murder. There were a number of high-profile cases towards the end of the twentieth century. Dr Nigel Cox was found guilty of attempted murder for injecting potassium chloride into an incurably ill elderly woman whose pain was intolerable, and who repeatedly begged him to end her life. Dr David Moor was acquitted of murder on the grounds that the high levels of morphine he gave to terminally ill patients were not intended to kill.

There have been many attempts to change the law, and MPs have been given a free vote on this, but the majority have always opposed it. Many doctors and nurses have serious concerns about legalising euthanasia, although surveys show that the general public supports it in certain situations.

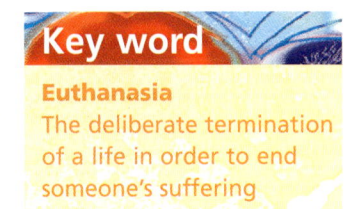

> **Key word**
> **Euthanasia**
> The deliberate termination of a life in order to end someone's suffering

# Decisions on life and living — Euthanasia

## Types of euthanasia

There are three types of euthanasia:

- **Voluntary euthanasia** is when a person asks a doctor to end his or her life.
- **Non-voluntary euthanasia** occurs when the patient is unable to request an end to life but it is believed to be in his or her best interests.
- **Involuntary euthanasia** happened in Nazi Germany. Sick and disabled people were killed without being consulted, though many were perfectly capable of stating their wishes.

### Key words

**Involuntary euthanasia**
Ending someone's life without his or her consent

**Non-voluntary euthanasia**
Ending the life of a sick person who is incapable of requesting death

**Voluntary euthanasia**
Ending a person's life at his or her request

Diane Pretty lost a court battle for the right to commit assisted suicide

If voluntary euthanasia were legalised, it might be used in situations of:

- terminal or incurable and very painful illnesses
- degenerative diseases, which lead to loss of dignity and quality of life

If non-voluntary euthanasia were legalised, it might be used for:

- those in comas or incapable of communication
- severely disabled newborn babies
- people suffering from dementia

Effects of Christianity on Behaviour, Attitudes and Lifestyles

## Active and passive euthanasia

**Active euthanasia** is illegal in the UK. It is an action taken or withheld with the deliberate intention of ending someone's life.

**Passive euthanasia** is legal as there is no intention to kill. It may take two forms:

- A doctor gives a patient a pain-relieving drug such as morphine, knowing that the dosage will have to be increased as the patient develops tolerance of the drug, and knowing that it will shorten the patient's life. This is not illegal because the intention is to relieve pain, not to end life. It is seen as good medical practice and an example of the principle of double effect.
- Medical treatment may be withheld or withdrawn from a dying person on the grounds that it is wrong to prolong the natural process of dying. The intention is not to kill, but simply to acknowledge and allow the inevitable.

### Key words

**Active euthanasia**
Deliberately ending the life of someone who is seriously ill

**Hospice**
A place that provides care for terminally ill patients

**Living wills**
These tell medical staff about how patients wish to be treated at the end of their lives, should they be unable to communicate their wishes

**Passive euthanasia**
Letting a person die without medical intervention

## The Dignity in Dying organisation

Dignity in Dying campaigns for the legalisation of voluntary euthanasia and for **living wills**, in which people can state that if they have lost all reasonable quality of life and are incapable of making their wishes known, they want their lives to be ended. People from all spheres of society are members, including medical personnel and religious leaders.

## The Pro-Life Alliance

This is the first European political party to be based on pro-life principles. It campaigns for the right to life as fundamental, and for more **hospices** to be properly funded to provide first-class care.

# Decisions on life and living — Euthanasia

## Arguments for and against euthanasia

**Key words**

**Macmillan nurse**
A nurse who is specially trained in palliative care for cancer patients

**Palliative care**
Specialised care that relieves pain and distress

The arguments in support of legalising voluntary euthanasia are:

- People have the right to choose, and the right to autonomy up to and including death.
- Euthanasia provides a quick and humane release from suffering. In similar circumstances we would choose euthanasia for our pets.
- Death is easier to face if we know it will be painless and dignified.
- Living wills can remove anxiety about the future.
- The suffering of relatives is lessened, and so is the burden of caring.
- The burden on the state is lessened.
- Doctors need not fear prosecution for carrying out euthanasia.

The arguments against legalising voluntary euthanasia are:

- It is unnecessary in view of the great advances made in **palliative care** in hospices and by **Macmillan nurses** at home.
- It is impossible to be sure that an individual wants to die if he or she cannot communicate.
- We cannot know how we will feel about things in the future.
- The last weeks and months of someone's life are helpful to relatives as a time for sharing affection and adapting to the fact that the loved one will not always be there.
- Unscrupulous relatives might abuse the system.
- Euthanasia implies that life is disposable.
- There could be a 'slippery slope' from voluntary to non-voluntary and even to involuntary euthanasia. Non-voluntary euthanasia, including that for babies, is now practised in the Netherlands.
- Mistakes might be made.

A Macmillan nurse with a doctor. Macmillan nurses help people with cancer to enjoy a better quality of life

Effects of Christianity on Behaviour, Attitudes and Lifestyles

# Christian attitudes to euthanasia

All the mainstream Christian denominations in Britain have made official statements opposing active euthanasia. In addition to the general arguments given earlier, their reasons are:

- Life is sacred and God-given. Only he has the right to take it.
- Euthanasia shows a lack of trust in God's love and mercy.
- God gave humans dominion over creation and the right to make responsible decisions for themselves, but there are limits to autonomy. To take life in this way is to play God.
- The weak and vulnerable who are unable to speak for themselves should have special protection.
- Euthanasia breaks the sixth commandment — do not kill.

The Vatican Declaration on Euthanasia states that euthanasia is 'the violation of the divine law, an offence against the dignity of the human person, a crime against life, and an attack on humanity'.

Nevertheless, many individual Christians believe that euthanasia should be legalised. In addition to the general arguments listed earlier, their reasons are:

- Life is sacred, but not absolutely so. It involves more than biological existence, and quality of life matters, too.
- Terrible suffering and loss of dignity are not what God wants for people. To put an end to this is therefore working with God.
- God gave humans dominion over creation, which means being entrusted with responsible decision-making throughout life.
- Personal autonomy is a God-given right.

All Christians accept passive euthanasia if medical treatment would prolong the process of dying. The Roman Catholic Church opposes the removal of feeding tubes from patients in a **permanent vegetative state (PVS)**. Other Christians see artificial feeding as medical treatment and think it can be withdrawn.

### Key words

**Permanent vegetative state (PVS)**
An irreversible condition caused by the destruction of the neo-cortical area of the brain

## Decisions on life and living — Euthanasia

# Questions and activities

## Sample questions and answers

**1** Which kind of nurses are specially trained in palliative care?

(1 mark)

Macmillan nurses.

### Commentary

A 1-mark question requires only a simple answer.

**2** Explain the 'slippery slope' argument against euthanasia.

(2 marks)

This argument claims that you may start by allowing only voluntary euthanasia, but it will not stop at that. It's a bit like a snowball rolling down a hill, which gets bigger and bigger. Eventually all kinds of euthanasia will be allowed.

### Commentary

This question is worth 2 marks, so a developed point is needed.

**3** Why do Christians disagree over withdrawing feeding tubes from PVS patients? (4 marks)

Some Christians believe that this tube is a form of feeding, and patients always have the right to be fed. To remove it would be a callous act and tantamount to murder. It is a form of active, not passive, euthanasia. Other Christians, however, disagree. In PVS situations, all the tube does is prolong the dying. The person has no hope of recovery, and the feeding tube can be seen just as a piece of medical equipment. To remove it is responsible and compassionate, and an act of passive euthanasia.

### Commentary

This question requires two viewpoints to be given. Because each view is worth 2 marks, some development of points is needed.

**4** 'If Christians really believed in compassion, they would support euthanasia.' Do you agree? Give reasons for your answer,

Effects of Christianity on Behaviour, Attitudes and Lifestyles

showing that you have thought about more than one point of view. Refer to Christian arguments in your answer. (5 marks)

I don't agree with this at all. Life is sacred and precious in God's eyes. Giving someone a quality of life and the belief that his or her life has value right up to the end is far more compassionate than saying, 'Your life has no point. Wouldn't you be better off dead?' The hospice movement means that euthanasia isn't necessary. Pain can be relieved and death can be dignified. If the patient wants to die at home with family around them, Macmillan nurses are available to give support. It is also more compassionate for families, who will treasure those last weeks and days with their dying relatives instead of always wondering if they did the right thing, and whether the really important things had been said and done.

I can, however, see why some people would disagree with me. In his lifetime Jesus did what he could to remove suffering. He certainly did not try to prolong it. As palliative care was not available, he might have supported voluntary euthanasia, where someone suffering terrible pain from terminal illness just did not have the emotional strength to go on any more. After all, when our pets are ill, we take them to the vet to be put down, as we do not wish them to suffer further. Some people think that this compassionate and unselfish caring for animals should be extended to people. If the hospice movement did not exist, I might agree with this view. But it does, and so I believe that it is far more compassionate to give someone a reason to want to continue living.

## Commentary

This answer is totally focused on the question, which centres around compassion. It considers both sides of the argument and makes reference to religious views. All these features are essential if an evaluative answer is to gain full marks.

## Further questions

1 What is meant by the term 'voluntary euthanasia'? (2 marks)
2 Which Christian denomination supports voluntary euthanasia? (1 mark)
3 Explain how some Christians use the idea of quality of life to support the argument for euthanasia. (4 marks)
4 Explain how some Christians use the idea of sanctity of life to oppose the argument for euthanasia. (4 marks)

**Decisions on life and living** — **Euthanasia**

## Class activities and homework

### Euthanasia and assisted suicide

Your teacher will divide your class into groups and assign one of the following case studies to each group: Dr Nigel Cox, Dr David Moor, Diane Pretty, Tony Bland, Heather Pratten, Anne Turner. You will be given the materials you need or will be able to do your own research on http://news.bbc.co.uk by searching for the name of the person you have been allocated. Prepare a short talk for the rest of the class, explaining the issues and whether you agree with the actions taken. (Although assisted suicide is not the same as euthanasia, the arguments for and against it are much the same, and so it is useful to study cases such as Diane Pretty.)

Note down your own views on the case study you were given.

### The hospice movement

If possible, your teacher will invite someone from a local hospice to talk about the hospice movement. Make sure you have thought about this meeting beforehand and have some questions ready. If no speaker is available your teacher will suggest useful websites for you to research the aims and facilities of hospices.

Find out about the case of Miss B by using the search engine on http://news.bbc.co.uk. Do you think her life-support machine should have been switched off? Justify your opinion.

## Useful websites

www.bbc.co.uk/religion/ethics  Click on *Euthanasia*.
www.dignityindying.org.uk
www.hospiceinformation.info
http://news.bbc.co.uk
www.prolife.org.uk  Type *Euthanasia* into the search facility.
http://re-xs.ucsm.ac.uk  Click on *Ethical & Moral Issues*, then on *Euthanasia*.

# Section 5

# The environment

## Environmental problems

Environmental problems are a big issue today. Some, such as drought, were known to our ancestors but are now experienced more frequently. Others are new problems.

Global warming is intensifying droughts

# Decisions on life and living — The environment

- Acid rain affects water in lakes, streams and soil. In Scandinavia, for instance, many lakes are unable to support fish, and some of this is due to wind-borne pollution from heavily industrialised countries like Britain. Contaminated water and food may be partial causes of respiratory and digestive disorders in humans. Trees are affected, and in the UK well over 60% of trees have suffered damage to their leaves or loss of needles. Some of the most beautiful buildings in Europe are also under threat from acid rain.
- Smog harms vegetation and humans.
- Rivers and lakes are polluted by agricultural, domestic and industrial waste. This kills marine life, and is a cause of cancer and birth defects in humans. In some parts of the world, major rivers are little more than open sewers.
- The sea becomes polluted from oil slicks, the dumping of industrial and domestic waste, and acid rain. This leads to toxic algae that kill marine life and contaminate seafood, pollute beaches and damage wildlife.

Unusually severe rainfall in one day in July 2007 led to flooding in many parts of southern England including Oxford

- Toxic waste is buried in deep holes or with domestic rubbish in landfill sites, which may cause health problems for those who live nearby.
- Pesticides and fertilisers kill wildlife and contaminate drinking water and human breast milk.
- An increase in the greenhouse gases that we produce is leading to global warming. This may result in flooding and the erosion of coastlines and low-lying coastal areas, as well as more severe droughts, storms and hurricanes. There may be an increase in the number and size of deserts.
- Thinning of the ozone layer may damage all forms of life.
- Over-fishing, hunting and the destruction of the rainforests are leading to the extinction of some species. There are fears that certain species of plants and animals that have never been discovered will vanish. Destruction of the rainforest is also contributing to climate change.

# What can be done?

Some of the proposed solutions are so far-reaching and costly that they can only be achieved by international cooperation. However, not all nations wish to be involved. Some countries refused to sign up to the **Kyoto Treaty**, which was drawn up in 1997 and in which EU countries called for an 8% reduction in carbon emissions by 2012. The EU has also agreed on a 20% reduction by 2020. President Bush said this was not in the interests of the USA, and some developing countries said it was not fair to expect them to have the same restrictions as developed countries.

The EU has made an attempt to conserve fish stocks in the North Sea by the introduction of quotas. This is not popular with communities that depend on fishing for a living, and many fishing fleets have gone out of business.

Britain is slowly getting to grips with these issues. Recycling is becoming a feature of everyday life, with regular collections of glass, plastic and paper. CCTV cameras are being set up to prevent fly-tipping, and

> **Key words**
>
> **Kyoto Treaty**
> An international agreement to cut back on carbon emissions and deal with environmental problems. The USA is the biggest polluter but refused to commit itself

**Decisions on life and living** — **The environment**

industries that pollute the atmosphere or rivers with their waste are being prosecuted and fined. Several cities are proposing to follow London in introducing a congestion charge, to keep cars out of the city centre. Car manufacturers are cutting down vehicle emissions. Improved public transport and the provision of cycle lanes help to reduce car traffic. Some consideration is being given to the use of renewable and natural energy sources. For instance, in Sweden 50% of domestic waste is incinerated to heat homes. Tree planting and reforestation are being encouraged in order to conserve wildlife.

The Green Party is a political party that focuses on environmental issues. Environmental pressure groups such as Greenpeace and Friends of the Earth educate the public and encourage people to become more 'green'. Individuals, whether Christians or not, can contribute in a number of ways, as shown in Figure 5.1.

*The environment: what can individuals do?*

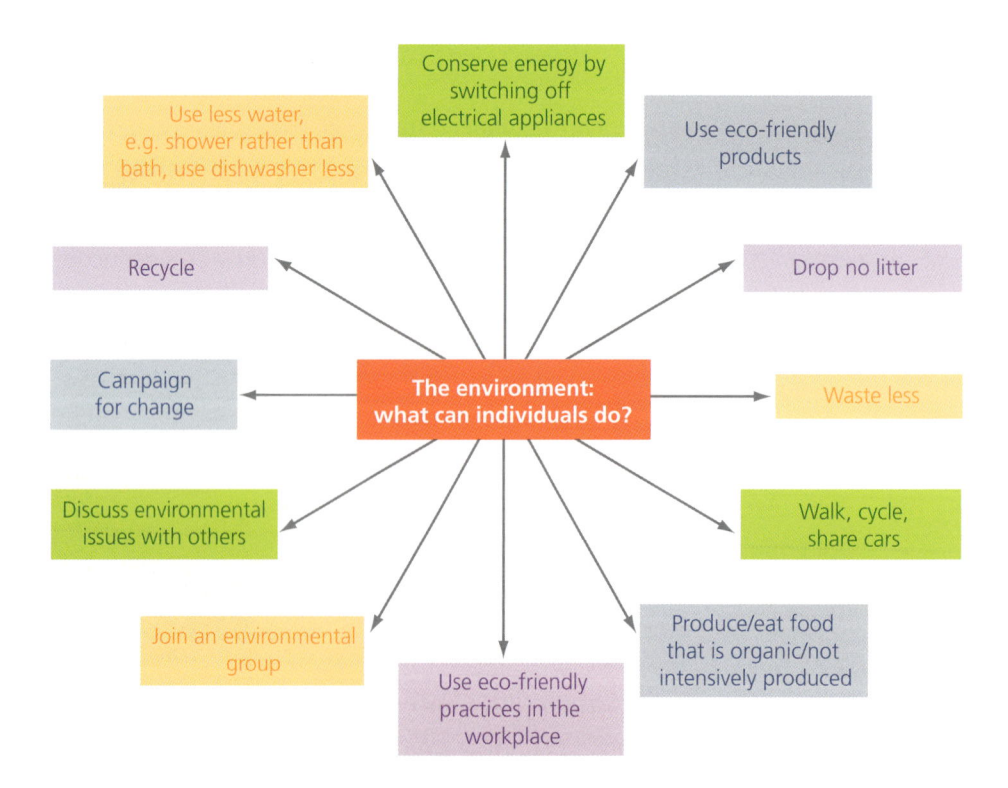

- Use less water, e.g. shower rather than bath, use dishwasher less
- Conserve energy by switching off electrical appliances
- Use eco-friendly products
- Recycle
- Drop no litter
- Campaign for change
- Waste less
- Discuss environmental issues with others
- Walk, cycle, share cars
- Join an environmental group
- Use eco-friendly practices in the workplace
- Produce/eat food that is organic/not intensively produced

**Figure 5.1** Individuals and the environment

Effects of Christianity on Behaviour, Attitudes and Lifestyles

# Christian attitudes to the environment

Christian principles relating to this issue are:

- **Stewardship** — the recognition that humans do not own the world but are entrusted by God with caring for it on his behalf
- **Responsibility** — because we are in a position of power, humans have a duty to conserve the world and everything in it

In the past, Genesis was not interpreted with sufficient care. It was believed that God created everything with humans in mind. The words 'fill the earth and subdue it' (Genesis 1:28) were understood in terms of domination rather than responsible stewardship. Most Christians now believe that Earth and the whole of the universe have intrinsic value. They see it as their duty to conserve the planet for future generations. They recognise that they have great power over the world and its creatures, but that this power must be used responsibly. Humans do not own the planet; it is on loan and they have the sacred duty of caring for it on behalf of God. He created the universe so it should be treated with respect. The idea of the sanctity of life extends beyond humans.

> **Key words**
>
> **Responsibility**
> The duties that humans have because of the power they exercise
>
> **Stewardship**
> Humans do not own the world but should look after it responsibly on behalf of God

Many Christians attend special services, such as harvest festivals, in which they thank God for his creation and for the produce they enjoy. They recognise the need to use its resources carefully. There are many hymns that celebrate the order and beauty of the universe.

A motion agreed at the Church of England General Synod urged the UK government to do all in its power to ensure that the Earth's resources were used fairly and economically, and to limit the damage caused by pollution. Many Anglican churches are now eco-churches with strict policies on heating and lighting.

*Christians attend services to thank God for the harvest*

## Decisions on life and living — The environment

The Christian Ecology Link was founded in 1981 as an interdenominational group that informs Christians about environmental issues. Charities like CAFOD, Christian Aid and Tearfund are involved with these as well as with global poverty.

In 1986, Christian leaders met representatives from other world religions at Assisi, the birthplace of **St Francis of Assisi**, to discuss environmental issues. They produced the **Assisi Declarations**, a set of statements on beliefs about the Earth and commitment to environmental conservation.

> **Key words**
>
> **Assisi Declarations**
> Statements relating to the environment made by leaders of world religions
>
> **St Francis of Assisi**
> Patron saint of animals and a role model for environmental concern

Many Christians are prepared to accept protest as a way of encouraging change, provided it is non-violent and keeps within the law. Some, however, see minor law-breaking such as trespassing or damaging property as justified in extreme cases. Christians who support this approach might point to the example of Jesus who overturned the traders' tables in the temple in protest at its misuse.

# Questions and activities

## Sample questions and answers

**1** What do religious believers mean by stewardship?   (1 mark)

Being entrusted to look after the world in which they live.

### Commentary
Only 1 mark is available, so a basic answer is sufficient.

**2** What is the importance of harvest festivals for Christians?

(2 marks)

At harvest festivals, Christians give thanks to God for the Earth and its produce, and recognise the need to conserve its resources.

### Commentary
A short answer making two basic points is sufficient for 2 marks.

## 3. Give three ways in which humans might look after the environment. (3 marks)

Recycling, not throwing litter, using less electricity.

### Commentary
There are 3 marks for three pieces of information, so three words or phrases are enough.

## 4. Explain why many Christians would disagree with the violent actions of some environmental activists. (3 marks)

The teachings of Jesus and Paul do not support violence. When he was being arrested, Jesus said that those who live by the sword die by it. Paul said that Christians should keep the law. Violence harms others, which goes against Christian beliefs.

### Commentary
The command word is 'explain', which means that 3 marks cannot be gained by writing a list. This requires one or two points with development.

## 5. 'What's the point in using my car less? One person can't make a difference to the environment.' Do you agree? Give reasons for your answer, showing that you have thought about more than one point of view. Refer to Christian arguments in your answer. (5 marks)

The problems facing our environment are so great that only total commitment to change by governments can save the world from total disaster. The evidence of climate change is there for all to see. Glaciers are disappearing, flooding is more common and hurricanes are more frequent and powerful than ever before. All countries have to make reduction in carbon emissions a national priority. One person cycling rather than driving to work is not going to achieve much, so what's the point?

Having said that, nations are made up of individuals and Christians believe that all individuals have a duty to live responsibly as stewards of the earth. We have all been entrusted with conserving resources by using them sparingly and not greedily, so that the Earth is the beautiful planet that God intended and so that our grandchildren can enjoy it. Even if one person cannot achieve much, it is still our duty to fulfil God's purpose.

# Decisions on life and living | The environment

I think the quotation shows a self-centred, lazy and defeatist attitude. What's to stop one individual getting together with other individuals and putting pressure on those in power to do something that will be effective? I believe that we live in an amazing world and I think it is up to each of us to keep it that way. The difference one person makes might only be small, but it's still important to make it.

## Commentary

This is an example of an answer where the person writing it feels strongly about an issue. There is no problem with that, providing the writer does not allow his or her views to make the response emotional or incoherent. If you feel strongly about something, you might find it helps to state the other side of the argument first.

## Further questions

1 Name a Christian organisation that campaigns on environmental issues. (1 mark)
2 Explain two environmental problems in the world today. (4 marks)
3 Outline the account of creation given in Genesis. (4 marks)
4 Explain how religious beliefs and teachings might affect the attitudes of Christians towards the environment. (5 marks)

## Class activities and homework

### St Francis of Assisi

Research and make notes on the teachings of St Francis that relate to the environment.

Find out what opportunities there are for volunteer work on environmental projects in the UK and elsewhere. Note information about two of these. You may use projects set up by secular or Christian organisations.

### Christians and the environment

Choose a quotation or statement relating to the environment from one of the Christian denominations you are studying. Create for display a poster using that quotation and display relevant images to get across the point being made.

## Your local council

Find out the ways in which your local council is committed to improving the environment. Make a list of what it does. Make another list of anything else you think it should be doing. It may be possible for your teacher to arrange for a local councillor to come in and answer your questions.

Create a 10-point action plan on ways of making your school or college a 'greener' community.

## Useful websites

www.arcworld.org  Click on *Projects*, then on *Sacred Gifts: WWF* to gain access to Christian environmental projects.

www.christian-ecology.org.uk

www.cofe.anglican.org  Click on *Shrinking the footprint*.

www.methodist.org.uk  Click on *Open to the World*, then on *Environment*.

www.reep.org.uk

www.request.org.uk  Click on *main site*, then on *basics* for a simple explanation of Christian attitudes to the environment.

# Section 6

# Biblical passages

## Creation: Genesis 1:1–2:3

This story states that God was the sole creator of the universe, bringing order out of chaos. He created it over a period of 6 days:

- Day 1: distinction between night and day through the creation of light.
- Day 2: creation of the sky.
- Day 3: creation of the earth with vegetation, and the oceans.
- Day 4: creation of the sun, moon and stars.
- Day 5: creation of aquatic creatures and birds.
- Day 6: creation of land animals, culminating in the special creation of human beings (both male and female) in the image of God and with power over all other creatures.

On the seventh day God created the Sabbath — a day of rest — to celebrate the completion of his creation.

Throughout this account, it is repeated that God was pleased with everything he had created.

Whether or not Christians believe that this story is literally true, there are a number of points to consider:
- The universe is ordered and good.
- Humans are in a position of power. However, this means stewardship and responsibility, not exploitation.
- Humans reflect the nature of God in a unique way — in their ability to think things through logically and to make informed decisions, in their capacity for deep and intimate relationships and in their creative powers.
- Because humans are made in the image of God, human life is sacred. Some Christians extend the idea of sanctity of life to the whole of creation.

# The Ten Commandments: Exodus 20:1–17

The Ten Commandments were given to Moses on Mt Sinai. God reminded Moses that he was the one who had delivered the Israelites from slavery and then gave the following commandments:
- Worship only God.
- Do not make any images of God.
- Do not use God's name for empty or evil purposes.
- Keep the Sabbath holy.
- Honour your mother and father.
- Do not kill.
- Do not commit adultery.
- Do not steal.
- Do not make false accusations or give false evidence about anyone.
- Do not covet, i.e. greedily and obsessively desire the possessions of others.

Mt Sinai, where Moses was given the Ten Commandments

GCSE Religious Studies AQA (A) Option 2A

The first four of these ten commandments relate to an individual's relationship with God. The rest are concerned with family and social relationships. The sixth and eighth commandments in particular have been applied to a variety of issues, such as:
- Are abortion and euthanasia tantamount to murder?
- Is exploitation of the environment a form of theft?

# Adultery and divorce: Matthew 5:27–32

Jesus extended the commandment not to commit adultery to include the thoughts and desires behind the act:

> But I tell you that anyone who looks at a woman lustfully has already committed adultery with her in his heart.

He also said that those whose right eye or hand was a cause of sin should cut it off and throw it away. Finally he commented on the Jewish law that, in order to divorce a woman, it was necessary to give her written documentation. In his view, divorce for any reason other than unfaithfulness would make the ex-husband guilty of causing her to commit adultery if she remarried. The man who married her would also be committing adultery.

A number of points need to be considered:
- Some Christians see Jesus's statement as referring to the desire to possess another man's wife or to unnatural sexual obsession, and not to the normal sexual desire felt by most men towards women in general.
- Jesus's second statement about losing a part of your body is not intended to be taken literally. It is a metaphor about irresistible temptation. People should steer clear of things that would end in disaster.
- Some Christians believe that Jesus's teaching on divorce and remarriage was an ideal rather than a rule.

# The body as a temple: 1 Corinthians 6:18–20

In his letter to the Christians of Corinth, Paul warned them to avoid sexual immorality as this had a profound effect on the individual concerned. The body should be seen as sacred:

> Do you not know that your body is a temple of the Holy Spirit, who is in you, whom you have received from God?

In other words, people should use their bodies for God's glory — their bodies belong to him.

This passage is useful for discussions relating to the sanctity of life or extra-marital sex. It raises the following questions:

- Is sexuality a purely physical thing or does it go deeper?
- Does the concept of the body as a temple of God apply to humans from conception? If so, does it mean that the embryo or foetus must never be harmed in any way or for any reason?

# Husbands and wives: Ephesians 5:21–33

Paul stated that wives should obey their husbands, who were in the same position of authority over them as Christ was in relation to the Church. At the same time, husbands must show the same self-sacrificial love to their wives that Christ showed the Church when he gave his life for it. Indeed, in loving his wife, a husband is showing self-love. Paul quoted Genesis 2:24, which says that the purpose of marriage is for two people to become one physically and spiritually.

> However, each one of you also must love his wife as he loves himself, and the wife must respect her husband.

Marriage is now seen as a partnership

## Decisions on life and living — Biblical passages

Many Christians reject this teaching, claiming it is outdated:
- Marriage is now seen as a partnership.
- Men and women are equals, with the same rights and responsibilities.
- The comparison between married love and that of Christ for the Church seems artificial and meaningless.

More fundamentalist Christians, however, might disagree:
- The teaching of the New Testament was directly inspired by God, so is always true.
- Someone has to take the lead in marriage.
- Men and women play an equal part in the marriage relationship but have different roles, which is reflected in the husband's position of authority.

# Justice and reconciliation

# Section 7

# Introduction

This short section is an introduction to the next two sections, which deal with crime and punishment, and war and peace. You must study both these topics in relation to the following Christian principles:

- justice
- reconciliation
- peace
- forgiveness

## Justice

**Justice** was a major concern to the biblical writers and it is still important to Christians today. It means that each individual has the right to fair, equal and respectful treatment.

**Key word**

**Justice**
Treating everyone fairly and equally

With regard to crime and punishment, justice applies to both the victim and the offender. The victim should feel that the hurt or loss he or she has suffered has been taken fully into account. The offender has the right to a fair trial, to being presumed innocent until proved guilty and, if convicted, to a fair punishment. Justice may mean that punishment has to be given, but it should not be seen as a form of revenge.

Justice is important in relation to war and peace. In modern times, the 'just' war theory applies the idea of justice to conflict situations. However, pacifists argue that war is always unjust.

Effects of Christianity on Behaviour, Attitudes and Lifestyles

# Reconciliation

Reconciliation means making up with someone. It is not always easy, especially if you are the one who has been hurt, but Jesus's teaching stresses this principle. Christians believe that his death on the cross was the supreme act of reconciliation, tearing down the barrier of sin that separated God and humanity.

Christians believe that any punishment should make reconciliation possible. Some forms of punishment are more likely to achieve this than others. The process of reconciliation leads to the healing of wounds and the possibility of moving on. This has been seen especially in the work of South Africa's Truth and Reconciliation Commission, where people who committed terrible crimes in the apartheid period met up with their victims. It is also seen in the restorative justice programmes used in some areas of the UK, in which victims of crime have the opportunity to meet those responsible, both to find out why the crime was committed and to make the offender understand the hurt caused.

The Community of the Cross of Nails, an international movement of reconciliation, was started as a result of the bombing of Coventry Cathedral

# Justice and reconciliation — Introduction

Christians argue that reconciliation plays an important part in preventing war and healing emotional wounds after a conflict. For example, when Coventry Cathedral was bombed by the German air force in 1940, there was no desire for revenge and no bitterness on the part of the cathedral staff. Two pieces of charred wood that had fallen in the shape of a cross were set up in the ruined building, with the words 'Father, forgive'. It is still there today. At the end of the war, nail crosses were sent as symbols of reconciliation to three German cities that the UK and its allies had bombed.

## Peace

> **Key word**
>
> **Forgiveness**
> Pardoning someone for what they have done and not holding it against them
>
> **Peace**
> Being able to live without fear of harm and to fulfil your potential

The hope for **peace** is found often in both the Old and New Testaments. The prophet Isaiah longed for an end to conflict and injustice, and the establishment of peace: 'Nation will not take up sword against nation…' (Isaiah 2:4). Jesus himself said to his disciples, 'Peace I leave with you…' (John 14:27). Peace is more than just an absence of fighting; it is a state of well-being, of spiritual wholeness. Peace means all people having the right to develop their potential, free from fear of harm.

Christians seek to create a society where people are able to live secure and fulfilled lives. Prison chaplains try to work with inmates, enabling them to come to terms with what they have done, to regret the hurt it caused others and to make a fresh start in which they are at peace with themselves and society.

Pacifists believe that peace means never engaging in conflict, which can be achieved only by finding other ways of dealing with a dispute. Others, however, think that war is sometimes the lesser of two evils and that it can be the only way of establishing long-term peace.

## Forgiveness

People often misunderstand what is meant by **forgiveness**. They think it is the same as forgetting what has happened. Methodist preacher Gordon Wilson publicly forgave the IRA terrorists whose bomb at the Enniskillen Remembrance Day ceremony killed his daughter, Marie. Gordon never forgot his daughter, but he was able to forgive her killers. Some people think that forgiving a murderer means not handing out punishment, which again seems wrong, especially if the

Effects of Christianity on Behaviour, Attitudes and Lifestyles

killing was coldly planned beforehand. Some form of punishment may be right and may be needed if justice is to be done. However, forgiveness can affect how the punishment is carried out and how the person being punished feels.

Forgiveness means a variety of things. For many, it is an ongoing process that may include recurring anger about the hurt that has been caused. It can also mean a refusal to seek revenge or to let hatred fester inside oneself. It means a willingness to move on instead of being locked into a cycle of bitterness.

For Christians, forgiveness is at the heart of their faith. Jesus said that God forgives unconditionally. To be in a position to receive that forgiveness, people must themselves be willing to forgive. As he was nailed to the cross, Jesus asked God to forgive his executioners.

# Questions and activities

## Class activities and homework

### Forgiveness

Your teacher will divide your class into pairs and assign to each of you one of the people featured on the Forgiveness Project website (www.theforgivenessproject.com). Prepare a short talk for the rest of the class on the experiences of the person or group assigned to you, explaining what the word 'forgiveness' means in that situation.

### Justice and peace

Think about how justice and peace go together. It might help you to read Isaiah 2:2–4; 9:6–7; 11:2–9. Create a poster to express your ideas.

Make notes on either the International Centre for Reconciliation (ICR) or the Community of the Cross of Nails (CCN).

## Useful websites

www.coventrycathedral.org.uk  Click on *International Ministry*, then on *ICR* or *CCN*.
www.crossofnails.org
www.theforgivenessproject.com

# Section 8

# Crime and punishment

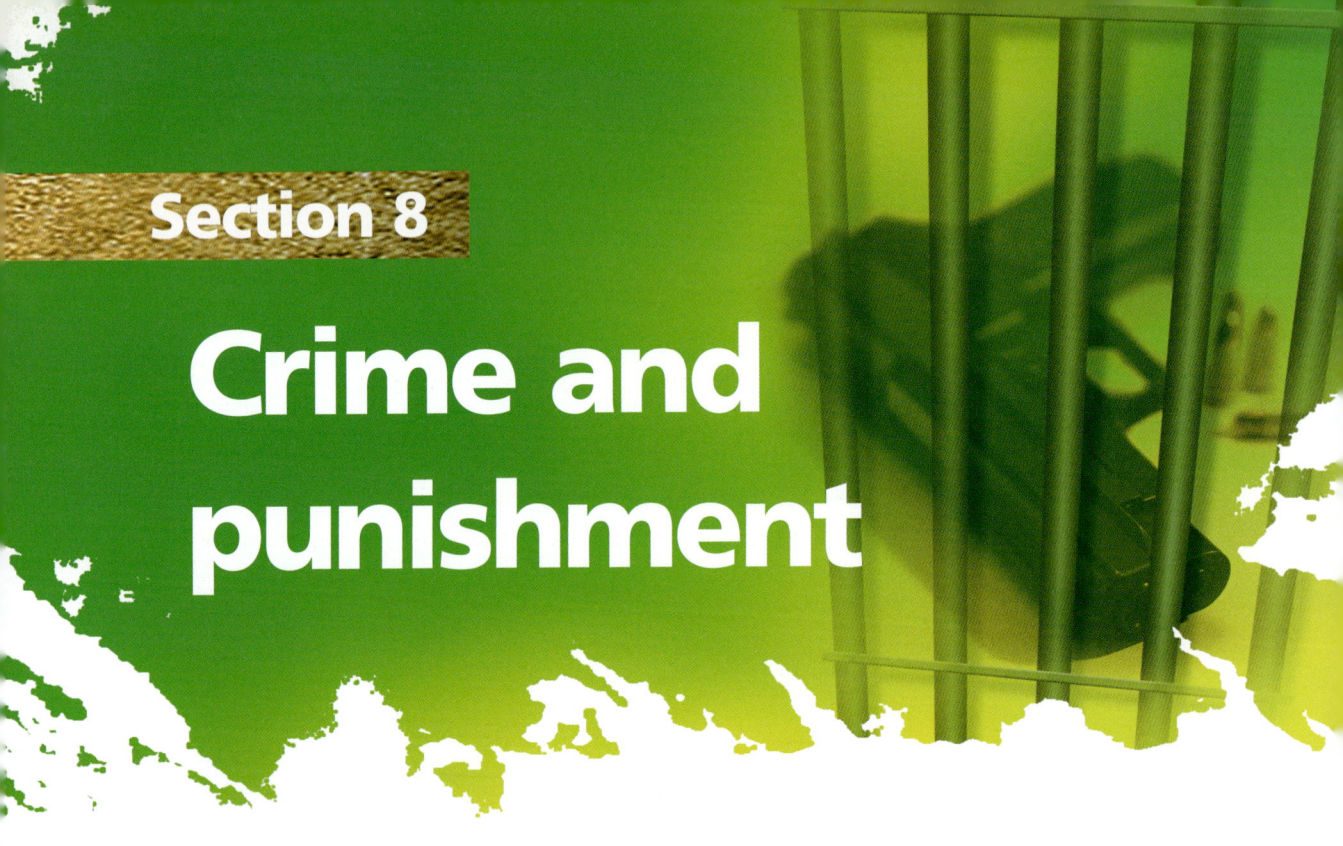

## Crime and sin

A **crime** is an offence committed in breach of the law of the land. Crimes may be committed against:
- a person, e.g. grievous bodily harm (GBH)
- property, e.g. vandalism
- the state, e.g. treason

Crime is a problem in Britain. The rate of recorded crime is dropping, but violent crime and robbery are on the increase. Men are far more likely to commit crime than women, and most criminals are in their late teens.

### Key words

**Crime**
An offence committed against the law of the land

**Sin**
A religious offence

A **sin** is a religious offence. It may also be a crime but there are many sins that it would be impossible or unfair to prosecute especially as Britain is a multi-cultural society including people of many faiths or no faith. A sin in one faith is not necessarily a sin in another and, in some religions, ideas about sin change over time.

Effects of Christianity on Behaviour, Attitudes and Lifestyles

## Why do people commit crime?

The reasons for committing crime are usually:
- social — the community someone mixes with or is influenced by
- environmental — someone's background and circumstances
- psychological — someone's personality and emotional state

There is debate about whether crime is a result of 'nature' or 'nurture', i.e. whether people are born with a tendency to be good or bad, or whether it depends on how they are brought up. Some experts claim to have found a 'gene for crime', which means that those who possess it may be more likely to break the law. Those working on the Human Genome Project (a project that is mapping out the entire genetic structure of humans) say that there are not enough genes in humans to programme our behaviour. This would suggest that environmental influences and our experiences as we grow up are at least as important as our genetic makeup. Many people would also argue that free will plays a part.

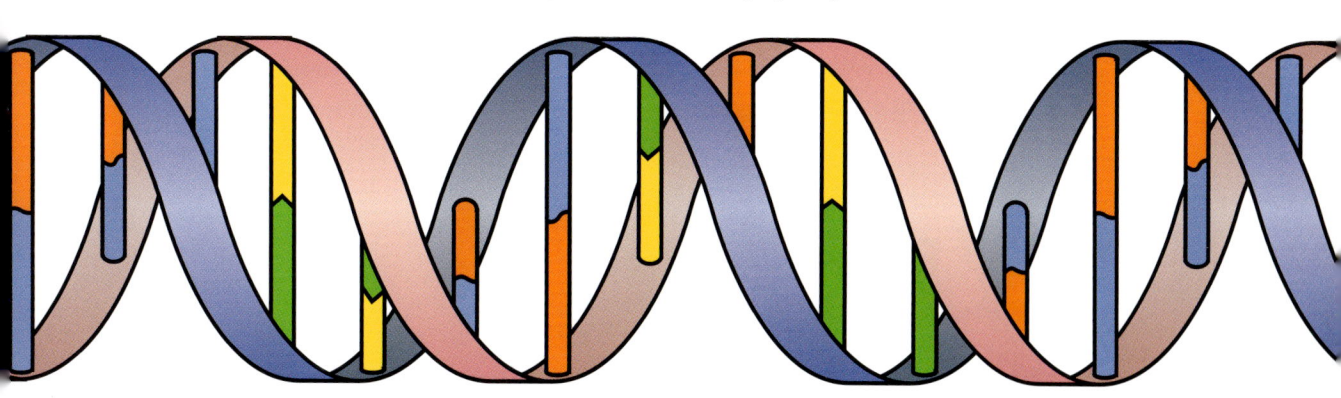

Some of the causes of crime are:
- alcohol and drug addiction
- poverty
- boredom
- peer pressure
- bad parental example
- emotional reactions such as anger or jealousy
- rebellion
- greed

Is there a gene for crime?

Justice and reconciliation — Crime and punishment

# Aims of punishment

Those who are found guilty of offences are usually punished. Before deciding on a particular punishment magistrates and judges think about why they are giving it and what they hope to achieve by it. What purpose does it serve? There are six aims of punishment:

- **Deterrence** — when a punishment is given to discourage the offender from committing crime again, and to discourage others who might be tempted to commit the same crime.
- **Protection** — law-abiding people need to feel safe. Victims of crime and frail or elderly people often feel insecure. Sometimes offenders with a mental illness need to be kept in secure accommodation in order to prevent them from committing an offence.
- **Reformation** — changing offenders' attitudes towards themselves and others so they no longer want to offend, but to contribute to society in a positive way.
- **Retribution** — often summed up in the biblical phrase 'an eye for an eye'. Retribution means giving a punishment proportionate to the crime. However, it can easily slide into revenge.
- **Vindication** — a fair punishment shows the offender and society as a whole that the law is just and must be respected. Those who break the law will be punished.

# Forms of punishment

Different punishments are available, depending on:
- the severity of the crime
- the nature and circumstances of the offender

## Imprisonment

The prison rate is higher in Britain than anywhere else in Europe and overcrowding is a serious problem. Conditions in many prisons are terrible, and some prisoners have to 'slop out' (empty chamber pots). Prisoners may be locked up for almost the whole time, with limited exercise and few opportunities for education or work. Bullying and assault are major issues, and suicide, attempted suicide and self-harm are common. The reoffending rate is high.

Young people who need to be kept in custody may be put in:
- young offender institutions (YOIs)
- secure training centres
- secure children's homes

## Parole

A parole board decides whether prisoners may be given early release. Levels of danger, likelihood of reoffending and attitude are taken into account. Offenders given early release have to meet regularly with a parole officer, who helps with their rehabilitation into society. They may have electronic tagging or curfew orders. At the end of a specified period, offenders are given total freedom if they have kept to the conditions. Any breach of conditions means a return to prison.

## Probation

As an alternative to prison, offenders might be assigned to a probation officer for a set period. During this time, they have to meet the officer regularly. Offenders have to remain in the area they live in unless given permission to move by the probation officer. If the terms of the probation order are breached, the offender is taken back to court for re-sentencing. Probation orders may be combined with other orders, such as a community service order.

## Community service

Community service is one of the many supervision orders that benefits the community. Offenders have to do unpaid work in their own time for a set number of hours.

## Fines

These are paid to the court and are given for motoring and some other offences.

## Electronic tagging and curfews

These are intended to help the police monitor the whereabouts of offenders and restrict their movements.

**Justice and reconciliation** | **Crime and punishment**

## Anti-social behaviour orders (ASBOs)

ASBOs are imposed to prevent someone from being in a certain area where they have been a nuisance in the past. For instance, persistent shoplifters might be banned from a shopping centre.

Persistent offenders may be given an ASBO

# Capital punishment

In 1965 **capital punishment** for murder was suspended for 5 years. In 1970 it was abolished. Technically, those who committed treason could have been executed, but none were, and now that penalty has gone, too. As a member state of the European Union, Britain is committed to a policy of not having a death penalty. Nevertheless, if it were put to a public referendum, the majority of British citizens would almost certainly support the death penalty for certain types of murder.

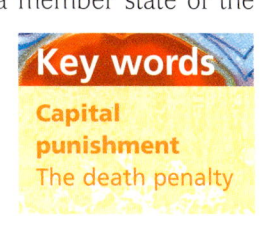

> **Key words**
> Capital punishment
> The death penalty

Worldwide, countries are gradually abolishing the death penalty, though many do still use it, for example China and the USA.

## Arguments for and against the death penalty

Secular arguments for and against the death penalty are given below. Christians use some of them alongside more explicitly religious points.

Arguments in favour of restoring the death penalty:
- Society would be protected. 'Life imprisonment' is not usually lifelong.
- It would act as a deterrent.
- A victim's family can be satisfied that justice has been done and they can move on.
- It shows society's total abhorrence of murder and stops Britain from becoming uncivilised.
- It is a form of reparation. In a sense, the death of a murderer is compensation to society for the loss of one of its members.
- Improved forensic science makes it unlikely that innocent people will be executed.
- The death penalty is kinder to a murderer than a lifetime of prison and guilt.

Arguments against restoring the death penalty:
- Release from prison is always on licence, which means that murderers may be recalled at any time and their whereabouts are always known.

# Justice and reconciliation | Crime and punishment

- The example of the USA shows that the death penalty does not deter murderers.
- If terrorists were put to death they would be seen as martyrs.
- It can too easily become a form of revenge.
- There is a possibility of innocent people being executed. Forensic science is only as good as the scientists using it.
- It prevents repentance and reform. Some 'lifers' have made an important contribution to society.
- It reduces society to the level of the murderer and shows a lack of respect for life.
- It harms others, encouraging feelings of revenge in the victim's family and punishing the family of the murderer.
- It is costly because the legal processes, such as appeals, are expensive.

## Christian attitudes to crime and punishment

### The law

Christians believe that God created humans with an inbuilt moral sense, the conscience, but that a wide range of other factors lead to crime: **original sin**, abuse of free will, personality disorders and environmental influences.

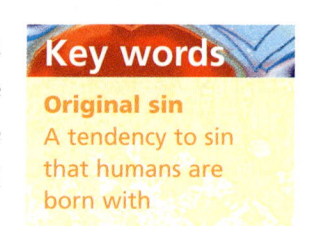

**Key words**

**Original sin**
A tendency to sin that humans are born with

All Christians believe that, to uphold a stable society, the law of the land should be obeyed unless it conflicts with the will of God as revealed in the Bible, the teachings of the Church and personal conscience. In the New Testament Jesus himself said: 'Give to Caesar what is Caesar's and to God what is God's' (Mark 12:17). Jesus clearly thought that there were duties to the state.

When there is a conflict between duties to the state and to God, Christians have taken Jesus's words as meaning that God should come first. There are examples throughout history of Christians taking a stand against unjust governments, for example Martin Luther King Jr in the USA, Dietrich Bonhoeffer in Nazi Germany, Oscar Romero in El Salvador and Desmond Tutu during apartheid in South Africa.

Effects of Christianity on Behaviour, Attitudes and Lifestyles

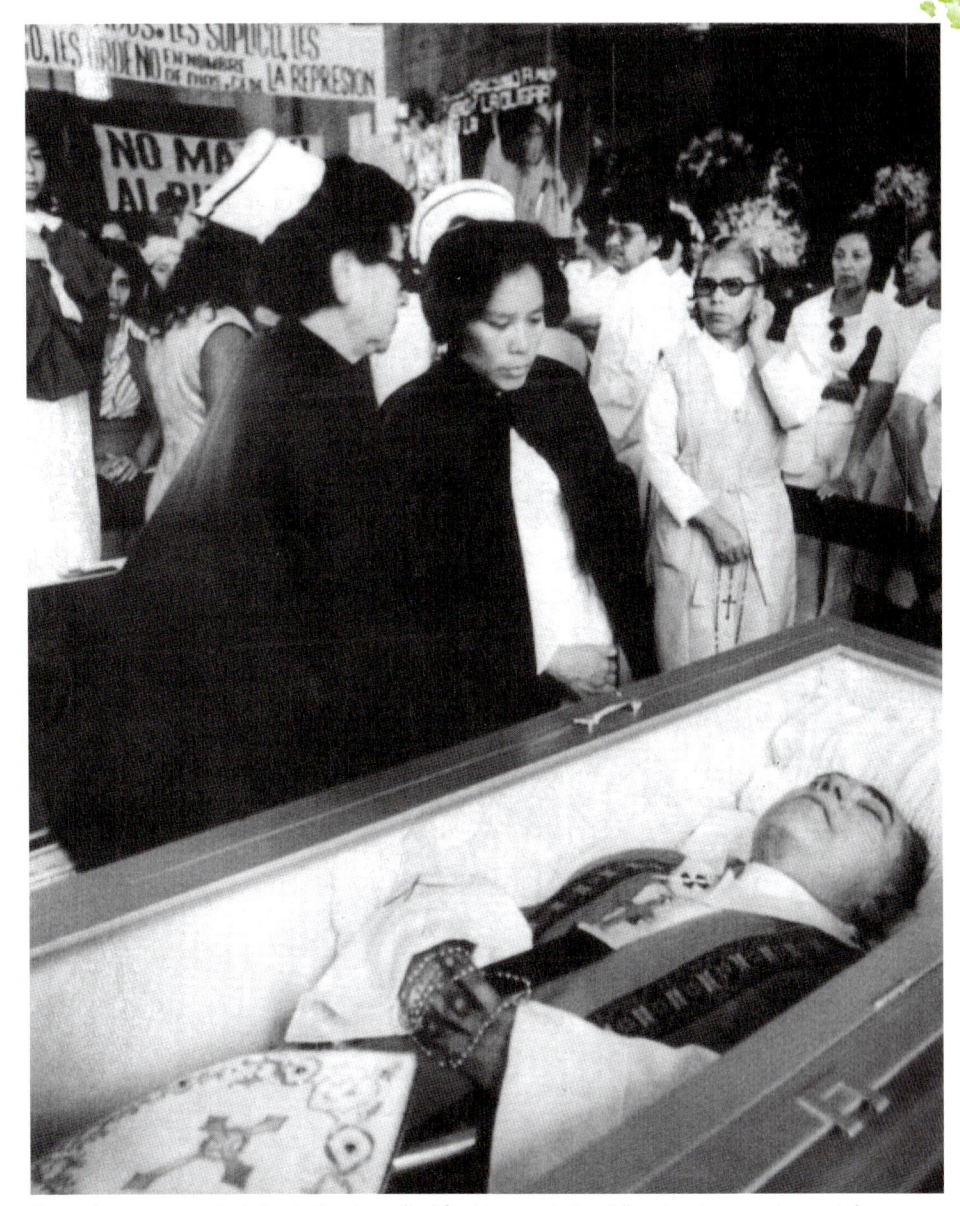

Oscar Romero was shot dead after he called for his country's soldiers to stop carrying out the government's repression

## Punishment of offenders

Christians accept that punishment may be necessary. Crime hurts its victims, and offenders need to know that. They also need to learn respect for the law as guaranteeing the rights of others.

## Justice and reconciliation — Crime and punishment

Punishment should always go hand in hand with forgiveness, which is central to Christianity. In the Lord's Prayer, Christians ask God to forgive their sins as they forgive those who sin against them. Jesus told Peter to be prepared to forgive unconditionally and without limit, illustrating this in his parable of the unforgiving servant (Matthew 18:21–35). Christians believe that an unwillingness to forgive damages offenders who are sorry for what they have done and those who are unable to forgive. Bitterness, hatred and the desire for revenge can easily consume a person. Those who are willing to forgive are more able to move on.

For Christians, the most important aim of punishment is reform. People must work with offenders to enable them to change. Christians are conscious that crime is often the result of material or emotional deprivation, and the offender needs help as much as punishment. The process of reform may include the use of restorative justice. This is a programme in which the offender and the victim agree to meet.

The aim of punishment Christians are least happy about, therefore, is retribution. Some support it as enabling justice to be done and as giving criminals what they deserve. However, retribution can easily degenerate into a desire for retaliation and revenge. This is totally against the spirit of the New Testament. Paul told his fellow Christians never to seek vengeance. Reparation is important. It is part of the healing process for the offender, the victim and society as a whole.

Christians recognise the need to protect society from some individuals. These individuals may also need protection from their own worst instincts through restrictions placed on their freedom.

Attitudes to punishment as a deterrent vary. It seems sensible to have a punishment that will deter potential offenders but treating someone harshly to deter others seems like unjust exploitation. People are then 'frightened' into being law-abiding, and fear is not the most effective method of achieving something.

Christians believe in giving offenders a second chance and offering them friendship. Some write to or visit people in prison, or offer support and friendship to prisoners' families. Christian employers may be willing to give a job to someone who has been in prison. All prisons have chaplains. There are discussion groups, Bible study and regular services.

The Anglican Church supports alternatives to prison as a more effective method of rehabilitation and re-education. It stresses the importance of tackling the sources of crime, especially poverty.

## Capital punishment

Some Christians support capital punishment, following the Old Testament teaching of an eye for an eye and a life for a life. They believe that only the death penalty shows that the law is to be obeyed and respected. The Catechism of the Catholic Church accepts the death penalty for what it terms 'grave offences', but prefers 'bloodless' solutions. Many modern Roman Catholic leaders are totally against the death penalty.

Anglicans and Quakers strongly oppose the death penalty because they believe it serves no useful purpose and is inhumane. There is no possibility of reform or reparation. There is a story about Jesus being asked to pass judgement on a woman caught in the act of adultery, the penalty for which was to be stoned to death. Jesus said that someone who had committed no sin should throw the first stone. The woman's accusers left and Jesus told the woman that he did not condemn her, but she should not repeat her sin.

# Questions and activities

## Sample questions and answers

**1** Name two types of punishment that might be given by British courts. (2 marks)

Imprisonment and probation.

### Commentary
Two words are sufficient.

**2** Explain two reasons why people commit crime. (4 marks)

Some people commit crime as a form of protest, for example trespassing on Ministry of Defence land in order to get their anti-war slogans televised. A drug addict may steal something and sell it in order to pay for the drugs he craves.

GCSE Religious Studies AQA (A) Option 2A

# Justice and reconciliation  Crime and punishment

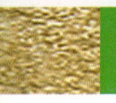

## Commentary

Two developed reasons are required here. The easiest way of developing a point is by giving an example.

## 3 Explain why many Christians are concerned about the state of British prisons. (4 marks)

Christians believe in the sanctity of life. All human beings should be treated with respect, but conditions in many prisons seem inhumane. In some prisons, 'slopping out' still occurs, which means that inmates have to use buckets in their cells as toilets. People may be locked up for 23 out of 24 hours because there are insufficient prison warders. This prevents the social contact that humans need if they are to function properly and makes prisoners feel frustrated. Imprisonment is meant to punish by removing a person's freedom; it is not meant to take away his or her dignity as a human being.

## Commentary

It would be easy to give a secular answer to this question, but that would not be awarded full marks because of the word 'Christians' in the question. There needs to be some religious content in the answer. This can be found in the first few sentences of the answer. The principle of respect for human life is then applied to the issue of prison conditions.

## 4 Explain the difficulties that an offender might face on release from prison. (4 marks)

An ex-prisoner might find it hard to get a job. This may be because employers are not prepared to trust him. It may be because he has served a long sentence and, even though he is qualified, he is not familiar with new technology and other developments in his profession. He may find it difficult to adapt to everyday life again. In prison, his choices were limited. His day was structured and almost every decision was made for him. On release, he may find the freedom and responsibility impossible to cope with.

## Commentary

Note the plural 'difficulties' in the question. This means that you must write about more than one problem. At the same time, the command word 'explain' and the allocation of 4 marks require more than a simple list of four difficulties. Development is needed.

## Further questions

1. When was the death penalty suspended in Britain? (1 mark)
2. Name two countries that still carry out the death penalty. (2 marks)
3. Name two crimes that are frequently committed in Britain. (2 marks)
4. Explain how Christian beliefs and teachings might influence the attitude of religious believers towards those who commit crimes. (5 marks)
5. 'Criminals should not be punished. Their genetic inheritance is responsible for what they do — they have a gene for crime.' Do you agree? Give reasons for your answer, showing that you have thought about more than one point of view. Refer to Christian arguments in your answer. (5 marks)

## Class activities and homework

### Capital punishment

Prepare for and hold a debate on the motion: 'This class believes that the death penalty is the most appropriate punishment for murderers.' Your teacher will divide the class into four groups, telling you whether you are to support or oppose the motion. One student from each group should present the arguments in the debate. Another student will act as chairperson. The rest of the class should be ready to make points arising out of the debate when invited to do so.

Make bullet-point notes on the most important issues raised in the debate.

### Organisations that work with prisoners

Your teacher will divide the class into small groups and will allocate to each group an organisation that gives support and help to prisoners. Prepare and give a short presentation to the rest of the class using any medium you wish, such as 'chalk and talk', a PowerPoint presentation or handouts. Use textbooks and leaflets provided by your teacher or carry out your research using the websites suggested below.

Research and make notes on the life and work of Elizabeth Fry, who was involved in the reform of Newgate Prison. What Christian principles motivated her work?

## Justice and reconciliation | Crime and punishment

## Useful websites

www.crimeinfo.org.uk

www.crimelibrary.com

www.howardleague.org

www.internationaljusticeproject.org

www.nacro.org.uk

http://re-xs.ucsm.ac.uk  Click on *Ethical & Moral Issues*, then on *Crime & Punishment*.

www.storybookdads.co.uk

www.theforgivenessproject.com

# Section 9

# War and peace

## Causes of war

Wars are usually fought to gain wealth or power, or for better trading opportunities. Sometimes wars are fought out of revenge, if a previous conflict ended badly for one side or the peace terms were humiliating. Many wars in the past were fought because of imperialism — the desire to conquer and rule as much of the world as possible.

Some modern conflicts have been ideological, to assert a particular way of life or set of beliefs. They may have political, nationalist or religious goals. Wars may be fought as a response to acts of aggression or to protect human rights.

## Consequences of war

Positive consequences may be:
- freedom from an occupying power
- the replacement of a corrupt government with a better one

Negative consequences may be:
- death — about 55 million people were killed in the Second World War and, in modern wars, most of those killed are civilians
- injury — again, the vast majority are civilians
- disease
- refugees

**Justice and reconciliation**     **War and peace**

- famine
- mental illness due to traumatic experiences
- kidnapping of children to be trained as soldiers
- destruction of relationships, culture, infrastructure and the economy
- hatred of the enemy and their supporters

In some wars, children are made to fight and kill

Effects of Christianity on Behaviour, Attitudes and Lifestyles

## The United Nations

The United Nations (UN) was set up at the end of the Second World War as a forum for discussing international issues. It was hoped to make war a thing of the past. Nations take their grievances to the UN and the member states try to find a solution.

The UN is occasionally involved in war although it does not have its own permanent army — member states supply the troops. One of its most important roles is the provision of peace-keeping forces, such as those in Lebanon in 2006. These peace-keeping forces are 'lightly' armed and may use minimum force if attacked or hindered from carrying out their duties by armed individuals or groups.

## The Geneva Conventions

The Geneva Conventions are a set of treaties that govern war and the treatment of prisoners of war. Most nations have signed up to the conventions, at least in part. Breach of these conventions is referred to the UN, and it may result in a war-crimes tribunal held in the Hague.

# Types of weapons and warfare

## Conventional

Conventional weapons range from bows and arrows to the most sophisticated computer-operated missiles. Huge amounts of money are spent on improving weapons and developing new types. Britain is a major arms exporter.

In recent times people have campaigned against the use of cluster bombs, which cause horrific injuries. At the end of the last century there was an outcry against the use of landmines. These are buried across large areas of land, often with no map to show their precise locations. Long after the war is over, they cause death or terrible mutilation, often to children playing in the fields or women going to fetch water. Princess Diana was involved in the Red Cross campaign against landmines, and she visited Angola in Africa to see the misery they cause. Britain has since banned their use, though companies can still make them for export to other countries.

# Justice and reconciliation — War and peace

Although state-of-the-art weapons can be aimed at specific targets to avoid killing civilians, sometimes mistake are made and civilians are hit.

## Atomic (nuclear)

In August 1945 the USA dropped atomic bombs on Hiroshima and Nagasaki in Japan, leading to the end of the Second World War in Asia. Hundreds of thousands of civilians died, radioactive gases are still present in the atmosphere and deformed babies are still being born. The USA justified this action by saying that it ended the Second World War more quickly. Today's nuclear weapons are much more powerful than those used in 1945 and their use would be devastating.

Many countries, including the UK, now possess nuclear weapons. They are believed to be a deterrent. The enormous threat that the weapons pose means that they are unlikely to be used.

> **Key words**
>
> **Campaign for Nuclear Disarmament (CND)**
> An organisation that supports unilateral disarmament
>
> **Multilateral disarmament**
> Nations disposing of nuclear weapons by mutual agreement
>
> **Unilateral disarmament**
> A nation disposing of its nuclear weapons regardless of what other countries do

Many people want to see the numbers of nuclear weapons considerably reduced and support **multilateral disarmament**. The USA and the Soviet Union did this towards the end of the twentieth century, although both countries still possess nuclear weapons in great numbers. Others are in favour of **unilateral disarmament**. This involves a country disposing of its nuclear weapons regardless of what other countries do. The **Campaign for Nuclear Disarmament (CND)** was set up in the twentieth century to protest against nuclear weapons. Opponents argue that to get rid of weapons would make a country vulnerable, but those who support unilateral disarmament claim that it would set a good example to other nations and encourage an atmosphere of trust.

The increasing number of countries developing nuclear weapons is a major concern, and there are fears that irresponsible governments or terrorists might obtain them.

## Biological and chemical

Biological and chemical weapons are banned under the Geneva Conventions, but both have been developed by many nations and used by a few. For example, in the Vietnam War the USA used napalm, which causes terrible burns.

# Terrorism

Terrorism refers to actions of extreme violence in pursuit of political aims. Sometimes terrorists target those they blame for injustice and oppression, such as the government of a particular country, but they usually extend their action to include innocent people. This is to achieve maximum publicity and terrify the public. Those motivated by religion believe they are doing God's will. Suicide bombers believe they will be transported to paradise immediately, without any wait for the Day of Judgement. Present-day terrorism is most commonly associated with:

- the **intifada** in Palestine
- Al Qaeda-linked groups, such as those responsible for 9/11 (New York) and 7/7 (London)

Most people claim that terrorism can never be justified because:

- The violence is indiscriminate and ruthless.
- It is a weapon of fear and coercion.
- It exploits the innocent to promote its purpose.

However, some people believe that on rare occasions there is no alternative to terrorism. For oppressed people who have tried every other means of putting right the injustice they suffer, such violence is seen as the only way of making the world take notice.

### Key word

**Intifada**
Palestinian uprising against Israel's occupation of their land

The destruction of the Twin Towers on 9/11

GCSE Religious Studies AQA (A) Option 2A

# Justice and reconciliation — War and peace

## The 'just' war theory

Although war is never a good thing, there may be occasions when it is justified. A simple form of the **'just' war theory** was in existence before the birth of Christ, but the Christian Church developed it over the centuries. It continues to be used as a standard by many people today, including politicians and journalists. There are eight criteria and each of them must be satisfied if the war is to be 'just'. In practice this is usually impossible so only the most important criteria need to be met.

For a war to be just, it must be fought:
- by a proper authority — a just war is one that has been declared by the ruler of the country concerned
- in a just cause — this is restricted to defence
- with right intent — the aims must be just and, once these have been achieved, the war must stop
- with reasonable chance of success — it is wrong for thousands to be killed in a war that has little chance of being won
- to ensure a better future than could be expected without a war — there is no point to a war if victory will not improve things
- as a last resort — everything possible must be tried to avoid going to war, such as talks, pressure from the United Nations and sanctions
- by just means — there must be no deliberate killing of civilians and the innocent
- with proportionate force — excessive use of force is not permissible

## Pacifism

Many people, including atheists and agnostics as well as religious believers, are **pacifist**. They believe that violence against other human beings is wrong. They are totally opposed to war, believing that it can never be justified.

Some of the arguments for and against pacifism are set out in Table 9.1.

**Key words**

**'Just' war theory**
Set of conditions to be met if war is to be justified

**Pacifist**
Someone who is opposed to violence

Effects of Christianity on Behaviour, Attitudes and Lifestyles

Table 9.1 Arguments for and against pacifism

| Arguments for pacifism | Arguments against pacifism |
|---|---|
| **Beliefs about human life**<br>- everyone has the right to life<br>- life is sacred<br>- lives should be treated with respect<br>- all are part of the human family | **The right to life is not absolute**<br>- an aggressor has forfeited that right by the act of aggression<br>- some lives may be sacrificed to protect others |
| **War causes immense suffering**<br>- modern methods of fighting harm the innocent<br>- the suffering caused is out of all proportion to the evil being fought<br>- the suffering may affect future generations | **War limits suffering**<br>- it can defend and protect the innocent<br>- the 'just' war conditions ensure proportional violence<br>- refusal to fight may make aggressors think they can do whatever they want, and this may result in more suffering |
| **War is a waste of resources**<br>- the money spent on weapons would solve social problems and meet some global needs<br>- money should be spent on saving lives, not destroying them<br>- it causes irreparable damage to the environment<br>- it uses up precious minerals and other resources | **War can be a wise use of resources**<br>- wars that are fought to end injustice may save resources in the long run because greedy oppressors waste resources |
| **War brings out the worst in people**<br>- e.g. greed and prejudice | **War brings out the best in people**<br>- e.g. courage and compassion |

# Christian attitudes to war and peace

In the early centuries, the Church was pacifist. Today one denomination, the Religious Society of Friends (Quakers), still is. Many Christians from other denominations are also pacifist and they may belong to a Christian pacifist group such as Pax Christi. One of the prominent figures in CND is Bruce Kent, who used to be a Roman Catholic priest.

Christian pacifists believe that everyone is a child of God and should never be harmed by a fellow human being. All humans are in the image of God and their bodies are 'temples of the Holy Spirit'. Life is a precious gift from God. Christians

# Justice and reconciliation — War and peace

quote texts from the New Testament, especially the Gospels, where Jesus encouraged forgiveness and reconciliation as the way to solve problems:

> You have heard that it was said, 'Eye for eye, and tooth for tooth.' But I tell you, Do not resist an evil person. If someone strikes you on the right cheek, turn to him the other also…You have heard that it was said, 'Love your neighbour and hate your enemy.' But I tell you: Love your enemies and pray for those who persecute you.
>
> (Matthew 5:38–39, 43–44)

When Jesus was arrested, one of his disciples took out a sword to defend him. 'Put your sword back in its place,' Jesus said to him, 'for all who draw the sword will die by the sword.' (Matthew 26:52)

Christians who are not pacifist believe that Jesus's teaching should not be taken literally. They point to Paul's letter to the Romans in which he stated that the civil authorities should be obeyed as their power was God-given. The Catechism of the Catholic Church states that while avoidance of conflict is the ideal, sometimes war is necessary. The Catechism supports the 'just' war theory, as do most other Christians who are not pacifist.

Dietrich Bonhoeffer was a German theologian who lived at the time of Hitler's rise to power. He was a devout Christian and a pacifist. He formed the 'Confessing Church', which opposed the government and helped to get Jews out of Germany. He was imprisoned and after his release he joined a secret resistance movement that planned the assassination of Hitler. He was arrested again and eventually executed in 1945, just a few weeks before Germany surrendered. In Canterbury Cathedral, Bonhoeffer is commemorated in a chapel dedicated to twentieth-century **martyrs**.

> **Key word**
>
> **Martyr**
> Someone who dies for his or her faith

All Christians, whether pacifist or not, are concerned about the arms race and the threat posed by nuclear weapons. Pope John XXIII spoke out against nuclear weapons and urged multilateral disarmament in 1963. An Anglican report called *The Church and the Bomb* encouraged unilateral disarmament, although the General Synod, the ruling body of the Anglican Church, voted against adopting its viewpoint.

Effects of Christianity on Behaviour, Attitudes and Lifestyles

# Christian attitudes to protest

Protest takes different forms and is carried out for a variety of reasons. Christians have been involved in protests against wars such as the one in Iraq. Christian Peacemaker Teams is an international organisation that gets involved wherever there is conflict. Members flew out to Iraq at the beginning of the crisis to try to encourage dialogue rather than force. Norman Kember was a human rights worker and pacifist. He went to Iraq to investigate human rights abuses and to draw the attention of the West to what was happening.

Another Christian, James Mawdsley, was involved in peaceful demonstrations against the attempted genocide being organised by the authorities in Burma. He was given a long prison sentence but was eventually released after pressure from the UK government. Two things inspired his demonstration: his deep Christian faith and his sense of justice.

From the 1960s there have been many demonstrations against nuclear weapons, particularly by members of CND, some of whom are Christian. They have been involved in a variety of activities and some were prepared to break the law by trespassing on government property. They believe that cutting through fences is justified. Most Christians, however, reject violent protest that harms other people either physically or financially (as a result of damage to property).

James Mawdsley is a Roman Catholic human rights campaigner

## Questions and activities

### Sample questions and answers

**1** Where was the first nuclear bomb dropped? (1 mark)

Hiroshima.

**Commentary**
Only the place name is needed.

# Justice and reconciliation — War and peace

## 2 Explain some of the possible consequences of war. (3 marks)

War may have positive effects on those involved as it could lead to a country regaining its freedom, which happened in Kuwait in 1990. On the other hand, war may have negative results. It often creates thousands of refugees and intensifies poverty. The refugees have no homes or income. If they flee to a neighbouring country, they have no rights.

### Commentary

Three consequences are given: liberation, displacement of people and poverty. The first point is developed with an example and there is further comment relating to the other two, which are linked.

## 3 Explain what Christians mean by a 'just' war. (5 marks)

For a war to be a just war, it must fulfil a number of conditions. One of these is that it must be fought in a just cause, i.e. it must be a war of defence. Britain went to war against Germany in the Second World War because Hitler invaded Poland. Poland was an ally, so Britain went to its defence. Another condition is that the war must be a last resort. Before war broke out in 1939, Britain had tried to sort things out peacefully. Neville Chamberlain returned from talks with Hitler waving a signed agreement. He believed he had secured 'Peace for our time'. When Hitler broke that treaty, it was felt that nothing other than war would stop him. Two other conditions are concerned with the way the war is fought: civilians should not be harmed and the amount of force used must not be excessive. Many people today think that these conditions were broken by Britain and the USA in the Second World War when the German city of Dresden was bombed and when nuclear bombs were dropped on Hiroshima and Nagasaki. Thousands of civilians were killed and extreme violence was used.

### Commentary

The command word 'explain' means that your answer should be more than just a list of conditions. Here, four conditions have been given, with examples to explain what the terms mean. In the last two sentences, an opinion (held by many people) is given, but it does not turn this into an evaluation question. The opinion is used to explain what 'just' and 'proportionate force' mean.

**4** 'Christians who go to war are hypocrites.' Do you agree? Give reasons for your answer, showing that you have thought about more than one point of view. Refer to Christian teachings in your answer. (5 marks)

I can see why some people think this. Christians of all denominations believe that peace is important and killing is never a good thing. The sixth commandment states 'Do not kill.' Many Christians are pacifist and believe that by refusing to go to war they are following the teaching of Jesus, who said 'Turn the other cheek' and 'Love your neighbour as yourself'. He told his disciples that those who live by the sword die by it, which means that violence creates more violence.

However, some Christians point out that 'do not kill' refers to unjustified killing such as murder, and believe that war entails killing in a just cause. Jesus said, 'Blessed are the peacemakers' and it could be argued that sometimes peace can be effectively made only through some use of force. For many Christians, war is never a good thing but it may be the lesser of two evils. They argue that religious believers who go to war are hypocrites only if they do so for selfish reasons and if they do it in a spirit of revenge. Personally, I think that it is not hypocritical to be involved in a war providing you keep the principles of your faith in mind and fight only in order to make something good come out of evil.

## Commentary

Two sides are discussed in some detail here. Note the instruction to include Christian teaching. Without this, the answer would reach no more than Level 3.

## Further questions

1. What is terrorism? (2 marks)
2. Explain how a Christian might apply the idea of sanctity of life to the issue of war and peace. (3 marks)
3. Explain why some Christians are pacifist. (5 marks)

## Justice and reconciliation · War and peace

## Class activities and homework

### Dietrich Bonhoeffer

In pairs or small groups, find out more about Dietrich Bonhoeffer. Imagine you are able to conduct an interview with him. With one group acting as Dietrich Bonhoeffer, think of some questions you might ask him. Your teacher will allocate roles so that each group has a different perspective. Possible roles are a member of the Nazi party, a member of Hitler's family, an ordinary German who sees Hitler as the 'saviour' of his people, one of Bonhoeffer's prison guards, Bonhoeffer's fiancée, a Christian pacifist, a Jew who escaped from Nazi persecution.

### 'Just' war theory

Find or write a summary of the causes, progress and ending of a particular war. Create a table with two columns, the first headed 'Just war' and the other 'Example'. In the first column, list the conditions given on page 80. In the second column, next to each of the conditions give an example from the war you have summarised showing how the countries involved fulfilled or broke that condition.

Find out about the work of the Campaign against Arms Trade at www.caat.org.uk. Research the cost of weapons and which countries are the major arms suppliers.

### War and peace film

Watch an entire film or clips from a film that raise issues of war and peace or civil disobedience, such as *Gandhi* or *Saving Private Ryan*.

### Christian pacifism

In pairs, research a Christian pacifist organisation and create a flyer informing the public about its beliefs and work.

Research in detail the life of a famous Christian who worked for peace by non-violent means. Use a sheet of A4 paper to show how he or she did this. Try not to give just a biography of the person, choose examples to show how he or she used non-violence to achieve peace.

Write a concluding paragraph to state whether or not you think he or she was successful.

Find out about and make notes on the work of a Christian individual or organisation that has been involved in protest.

## Useful websites

www.anglicanpeacemaker.org.uk

www.baptist-peace.org.uk

www.caat.org.uk

www.chipspeace.org

www.corrymeela.org

www.coventrycathedral.org.uk

www.cptuk.org.uk

http://news.bbc.co.uk

www.paxchristi.org.uk

www.quaker.org.uk

www.yap.org

# Section 10

# Biblical passages

## Teaching on forgiveness: Matthew 5:38–48

Jesus quoted two sayings (the first of which occurs three times in the Old Testament) and then commented on them.

The first saying, 'Eye for eye, and tooth for tooth' was intended to ensure that there was compensation for any harm done. However, Jesus said, 'But I tell you, Do not resist an evil person.' He used three illustrations from everyday life to make his point. If someone was given an insulting slap on one cheek, he or she should offer the other. If someone was in debt and being taken to court, he or she should offer more than the amount being demanded. If someone was forced to carry a Roman soldier's pack for a mile, he or she should carry it for two miles.

Some Christians understand from his instruction to 'turn the other cheek' that Jesus was a pacifist and that he would have always rejected any form of violence. Others think that this statement should be read metaphorically. They point out how it was typical of Jesus to use exaggeration to get his point across. In this instance he was telling his disciples never to seek revenge but to respond to evil in a positive way. However this passage is interpreted, it means that Christians should seek reconciliation.

*The Bible tells us to seek reconciliation instead of argument*

The second saying was 'Love your neighbour and hate your enemy.' Jesus went on to say, 'But I tell you: Love your enemies and pray for those who persecute you, that you may be sons of your Father in heaven.' He stated that God treats everyone alike; he does not favour those who are good. Jesus also pointed out that there is no virtue in being nice to those who are nice to you; it is human nature to behave like that. He told his disciples that they should try to be perfect, just as God is, and that meant treating everyone the same. This passage calls for an attitude of forgiveness. It is not possible to love your enemies without forgiving them.

# The unmerciful servant: Matthew 18:23–35

Jesus told this parable in answer to a question that Peter put to him. Peter asked how often he should be prepared to forgive someone who kept on sinning against him. Was seven times enough? Jesus said, 'I tell you, not seven times, but seventy-seven times' and then told the following story.

A king was settling his accounts and summoned a servant who owed him a huge amount of money — more than he could pay in a lifetime. He told the servant that he and his whole family would be sold into slavery as payment. The servant fell at his feet and begged for more time. The king felt sorry for him and cancelled the whole debt. The servant then went out and met a fellow-servant who owed him a small amount of money. He grabbed the man by the throat and demanded immediate repayment. He ignored the man's plea for more time and had him thrown into prison. This was reported to the king, who sent for the servant and rebuked him for not showing the mercy he had been shown. He was sent to prison until the debt was paid.

Jesus was explaining that if people wish to be forgiven by God, they should be capable of showing forgiveness themselves. If they cannot do this, it shows that they do not understand what forgiveness means.

## The arrest of Jesus: Matthew 26:47–53

While Jesus was in Gethsemane he was betrayed by Judas, one of his disciples. Judas kissed Jesus so that the soldiers knew who to arrest. Nevertheless, Jesus addressed him as 'friend'. When Jesus was arrested, a scuffle broke out in which one of Jesus's disciples struck the high priest's servant, cutting off his ear. Jesus rebuked the disciple, telling him to put his sword away: '…for all who draw the sword will die by the sword'.

Jesus clearly opposed violence on this occasion, saying that it led to more violence. Christian pacifists use this passage to support their view that war is never justified and that it makes things worse. Others argue that although what Jesus said about violence is true, sometimes there is no alternative.

Jesus's words could be seen as an argument that opposes seeking revenge against those who commit crimes. Some people say that receiving harsh treatment in prison makes inmates bitter and increases any violent tendencies they may already have.

## The traders in the temple: Mark 11:15–18

The outer courtyard of the temple was an area in which non-Jews could go to worship God. However, it was difficult to pray in that area as it was used as a place for selling animals and for changing Roman money. Jesus was angry about this and about the way people used the courtyard as a short cut from one part of the city to another. He drove out the merchants, overturning the tables and stools. He stopped people using the courtyard as a short cut. He said the temple was to be a house of prayer for all nations, adding, 'But you have made it "a den of robbers".'

This passage is used by Christians to justify the use of limited violence in protest. Jesus did not harm any individuals, nor did he damage property, but he certainly used force.

# The spirit of the Lord: Luke 4:16–21

When Jesus returned to his home town of Nazareth, he went to the synagogue where he was invited to read one of the lessons. He read the following passage from Isaiah 61:1–2:

> The Spirit of the Sovereign Lord is on me, because the Lord has anointed me to preach good news to the poor. He has sent me to bind up the brokenhearted, to proclaim freedom for the captives and release from darkness for the prisoners, to proclaim the year of the Lord's favour

Jesus rolled up the scroll, handed it back to the attendant and sat down, saying that that passage had now been fulfilled.

Christians believe that Jesus's mission was to bring justice and hope to the downtrodden. They also believe that it is their duty to ensure that the rights of all humans are respected. Some Christians think that violence is sometimes the only way of achieving this.

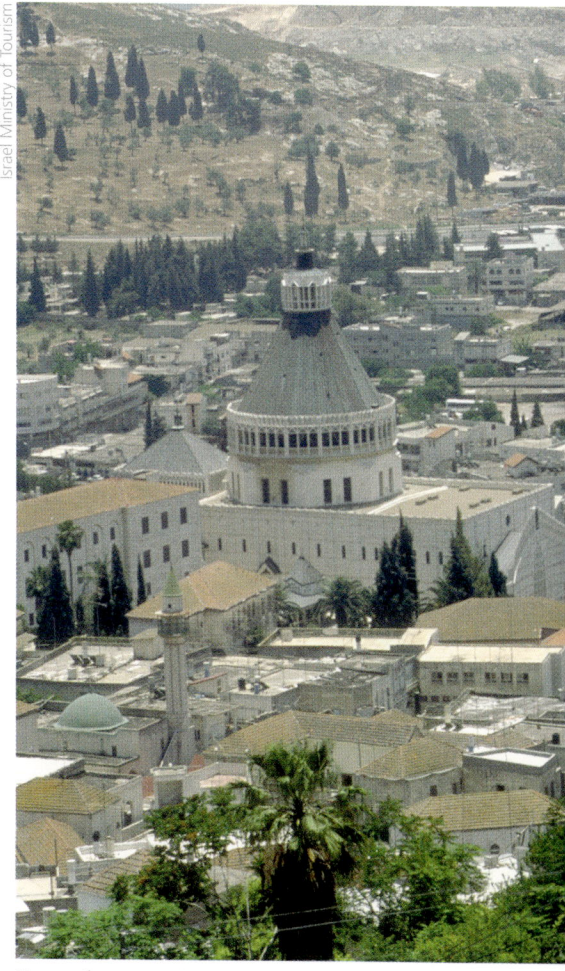

Nazareth

**Justice and reconciliation**     **Biblical passages**

# The forgiving father: Luke 15:11–32

Jesus, in response to criticism that he befriended outcasts and ate meals with them, told the story of a father who had two sons. The younger son could not wait until his father was dead to receive his inheritance — he wanted it immediately. So his father gave him his share of the family property. The young man went abroad with the money, which he quickly wasted. A severe famine hit the country, so he had to find a job. He ended up working as a swineherd — a job that no self-respecting Jew would ever consider. The pay was poor and he was hungry and miserable. He thought longingly of the home he had turned his back on, and how even the lowest workers there were well fed. He decided to go home. While he was still some distance from home, his father saw him and was filled with compassion for him. He ran to his son, hugging and kissing him. He told his servants to bring the best robe, a ring and shoes, and to kill the prize calf and prepare a feast.

The older son had been working in the fields. On his way home, he heard the sound of music and dancing and asked a servant what was going on. When he was told that his brother's return was being celebrated, he was furious and refused to go in. His father came and begged him, but the son angrily said that he had shown total obedience and loyal service for years but had never been given even a goat to feast on with his friends. Yet his brother who had squandered his father's property was treated to the fattened calf. His father simply replied, 'My son, you are always with me, and everything I have is yours. But we had to celebrate and be glad, because this brother of yours was dead and is alive again; he was lost and is found.'

The father was saying that he loved both his sons, and that everything belonged to the older boy. However, as a father, he was bound to be happy at the return of his younger son. Jesus was saying that God, like the father in the story, loves all his children and that his forgiveness is unconditional.

This parable teaches us that in God's eyes it is never too late for us to be sorry, and there is no limit to his forgiveness. Even the worst offender should be given the chance to make a fresh start, as Christians should reflect God's forgiveness in their attitudes to other people. They should not bear grudges.

# The penitent thief: Luke 23:32–43

As Jesus was nailed to the cross alongside two criminals, he asked God to forgive those responsible for his execution: 'Father, forgive them, for they do not know what they are doing.' The soldiers on guard duty gambled for his clothes and offered Jesus cheap wine, telling him to save himself if he really was the King of the Jews. Jewish leaders mocked him in a similar way, saying, 'He saved others; let him save himself if he is the Christ of God, the Chosen One.' One of those being crucified with him joined in the taunts, telling him to save all three of them if he was the Christ. The other criminal, however, rebuked the first one for saying this. He stated that they deserved their punishment, but Jesus was innocent of any crime. He then said to Jesus, 'Jesus, remember me when you come into your kingdom.' Jesus replied, 'I tell you the truth, today you will be with me in paradise.'

Christians use this passage as evidence that no one is beyond God's forgiveness and that it is never too late to repent of your sins. It is used as an argument against the death penalty, which does not allow the offender time to repent, seek forgiveness and make a new start. Jesus's words at the start of this passage encourage Christians to forgive those who hurt them and cause them harm.

A demonstration against the death penalty in Texas

**Justice and reconciliation** | **Biblical passages**

# The woman in adultery: John 8:2–11

Although it was rarely carried out, the punishment for adultery during Jesus's time was stoning to death. A woman caught in the act of adultery was dragged to Jesus for his verdict on what should be done to her. Jesus bent down and wrote on the ground with his finger. Perhaps he needed time to think, or maybe he was angry about the treatment of the woman and could not bring himself to speak. Perhaps he hoped that his silence would make his questioners think about what they were doing to the woman and go away. Whatever the reasons for his silence, they continued to question him. He stood up and replied, 'If any one of you is without sin, let him be the first to throw a stone at her.' He then bent down again and continued writing on the ground. His questioners slowly walked away until Jesus and the woman were alone. Jesus straightened up again and asked the woman if anyone had condemned her. She replied, 'No-one, sir.' Jesus then said to her, 'Then neither do I condemn you. Go now and leave your life of sin.'

Christians who oppose the death penalty use this passage to claim that no-one is perfect, and therefore no-one has the right to carry out the death sentence. However, Jesus was not condoning sin. He did not condemn the woman, but he told her not to commit adultery again. Christians sometimes talk about hating the sin but loving the sinner.

# The authority of the state: Romans 13:1–7

In his letter to the Christians in Rome, Paul told them that they should obey the civil authorities because their authority came from God. Opposition to the authorities was therefore a challenge to God. He stated that those in power were God's servants who worked for the benefit of their subjects, and only those who broke the law need fear them. He warned his readers that if they did wrong, they would pay for it. He said they should pay their taxes and show the authorities respect.

Christians obey the law and pay their taxes because they see responsible citizenship as a duty of all human beings. They believe that what Paul said is valid as long as the government is just and its demands are fair. However, if those in authority were corrupt, or if they made laws that went against Christian principles, many Christians would feel that they had to make a stand. Some might be prepared to resort to violence to overthrow a corrupt or tyrannical government.

Effects of Christianity on Behaviour, Attitudes and Lifestyles

# Christian responsibility

# Section 11

# Prejudice and discrimination

## What are prejudice and discrimination?

**Prejudice** means having negative opinions about others without any sound reasons. It is literally 'pre-judging'.

**Discrimination** is the unfair treatment of others on the basis of prejudice. Generally, discrimination is negative — discriminating against someone. It can, however, be positive — discriminating in favour of someone. For example, positive discrimination has been applied by some British universities. They favour students from deprived backgrounds or under-achieving schools over those from independent schools.

> **Key words**
> **Discrimination**
> Putting prejudice into action
> **Prejudice**
> An irrational opinion about an individual or group

## Causes of prejudice and discrimination

There are many reasons for prejudice and discrimination but the main one is ignorance. Lack of knowledge and understanding can easily lead to:
- fear through feeling threatened in some way

- **stereotyping** — thinking that everyone in a group has certain qualities (e.g. all football fans are hooligans)
- **scapegoating** — blaming certain groups for what is wrong in society

# Discrimination and the law

Although most forms of discrimination are illegal, it is still a problem in British society. The law might not give adequate protection if:
- the discrimination is subtle
- there are no witnesses
- witnesses are reluctant to give evidence, either because they do not want to be involved or because they fear some kind of backlash
- the discrimination is not reported because the victim is afraid of the offender seeking revenge
- the victim is not as articulate as the discriminator if the case comes to court/tribunal

The law cannot dictate how people think. It cannot control prejudice, which can easily lead to discrimination. Some people are brainwashed by the prejudice of others (e.g. parents or the media) into believing that the law should be broken. Extremist nationalist groups such as the **British National Party (BNP)** have been accused of encouraging prejudice and whipping it up into hatred.

### Key words

**British National Party (BNP)**
A far-right political party in the UK

**Scapegoating**
Blaming an innocent individual or group for something that is wrong

**Stereotyping**
Creating an oversimplified image of an individual or group, usually by assuming that all members of the group are the same

# Racial discrimination

Black people and other ethnic minority groups are more likely to be victims of discrimination than white people. It may take a number of forms:
- verbal abuse such as name-calling
- damage to property
- physical attacks
- problems in finding jobs or being promoted

# Christian responsibility                    Prejudice and discrimination

Stephen Lawrence

In 1993 Stephen Lawrence, a British teenager, was stabbed to death while waiting for a bus. He was murdered because he was black. The police investigation was highly flawed and those tried for Stephen's murder were acquitted. A public inquiry was held, which exposed the problem of **institutional racism** in the police force. Other public institutions, such as the armed forces and the Church, have also been found guilty of institutional racism. It is something that is deeply ingrained in much of British society and is not easy to deal with.

### Key words

**Institutional racism**
Racial prejudice and discrimination that are said to be at the heart of some organisations

## Laws relating to racial discrimination

The 1976 Race Relations Act bans discrimination on the grounds of racial origins in all key areas of life:

- housing
- employment
- education
- welfare

It is illegal to say or do anything that might stir up racial hatred.

The Commission for Racial Equality (CRE) was set up to monitor and deal with racial discrimination. In 2000 further laws were passed to prevent racial discrimination in national and local government, hospitals and schools.

Effects of Christianity on Behaviour, Attitudes and Lifestyles

# Gender discrimination

Victims of gender discrimination are usually women. Until the beginning of the twentieth century, women in the UK were regarded as the property of their fathers or husbands. Attitudes began to change during the First World War, when women had to do 'men's work'. The **Suffragette movement** aimed at extending suffrage — the right to vote — to women. In 1918 women over the age of 30 were given the vote (although men could vote at 21). Women were given the vote on the same terms as men in 1928.

**Key words**

**Suffragette movement**
A reform movement in the early twentieth century that aimed to secure the right for women to vote

Suffragettes were prepared to break the law to gain the right for women to vote

However, for several decades after gaining the right to vote, women were expected to stop working when they got married. It was only towards the end of the twentieth century that it became the norm for women to continue working after getting married and having children. Even then, some jobs were still seen as more suitable for men, but women can increasingly be found in what were traditionally male-dominated careers, such as engineering and the sciences.

Nevertheless, many women are still not paid as well as men and it may not be easy for them to get the most senior jobs. When they do, they often face resentment and harassment. Many women work part-time so that they can spend more time with their children, but by doing so they are especially vulnerable to discrimination.

## Laws relating to gender discrimination

The Equal Pay Act 1970 made it illegal for employers to discriminate between men and women in terms of their pay or conditions when they are doing the same or similar work. The Sex Discrimination Act 1975 made it unlawful to discriminate on the grounds of gender in:

- employment
- education
- housing, goods, facilities and services
- advertising

The Equal Opportunities Commission was set up to monitor and deal with gender discrimination.

# Disability discrimination

In the past, many disabled people were excluded from everyday activities. Those in wheelchairs often could not access public transport, shops, restaurants and cinemas. The needs of blind and deaf people were not met in the way information was given out. Disability sports such as the Paralympics were given no media coverage.

Much has changed for the better in recent years, but there is still underlying prejudice against disabled people that can lead to discrimination. It is often wrongly assumed that a disabled person is incapable of enjoying or contributing to life as much as someone without a disability.

## Laws relating to disability discrimination

The Disability Discrimination Act 1995 made it unlawful to discriminate on the grounds of disability in:
- employment
- provision of goods and services
- education

Because of the time and costs involved in carrying out the requirements of this Act (e.g. getting planning permission and making alterations to buildings), a long phasing-in period was allowed.

A more recent law has been passed to ensure that blind and deaf people have the same access to information as those whose sight and hearing are not impaired. For example, on trains both visual and auditory information is given about the journey. Timetables are available in Braille and on audiotape.

> **Key word**
>
> **Equality**
> The idea that everyone is of equal importance and value, and should be treated as such

# Christian attitudes to prejudice and discrimination

The following principles are central to Christian views on prejudice and discrimination:
- **equality**, which means that all human beings are of equal importance and value, and should be treated the same
- **justice**, which means that all human beings have the same rights to fair and equal treatment

Christians of all denominations agree that prejudice and discrimination are sinful. The Catechism of the Catholic Church expresses the Christian position clearly:

> Every form of social or cultural discrimination in fundamental personal rights on the grounds of sex, race, colour, social conditions, language or religion must be curbed and eradicated as incompatible with God's design.

Christians look to the example of Jesus, who was frequently rebuked for his friendship with outcasts. He was prepared to mix with and heal non-Jews, who were seen as unclean. He told a parable in which a Samaritan, whose people had long been bitter enemies of the Jews, was a hero.

**Christian responsibility** — **Prejudice and discrimination**

Perhaps the most famous statement on equality comes from Paul: 'There is neither Jew nor Greek, slave nor free, male nor female, for you are all one in Christ Jesus' (Galatians 3:28). On another occasion, Paul said, 'From one man he made every nation of men, that they should inhabit the whole earth…' (Acts 17:26).

Although some Christians played a leading role in abolishing the slave trade, others owned slaves. In the UK today there are few black or Asian priests. However, in 2006 the first black Archbishop of York, John Sentamu, was consecrated and many Anglicans see this as a sign that the Church can now transcend barriers of race and culture. The Church of England has a committee that deals with issues affecting people of other races, e.g. immigration and unemployment.

John Sentamu is the first black archbishop in the UK

Unfortunately, Christianity also has a history of discrimination against women. In the early centuries of the Church, a Church council decided by a majority of one that women were human beings! For centuries women were seen as just housekeepers and child-bearers. Throughout history, the Church has also had influential

Effects of Christianity on Behaviour, Attitudes and Lifestyles

female role models such as Hildegard of Bingen, Catherine of Siena and Mother Julian of Norwich. In 1944 Li Tim-Oi was the first female priest to be ordained in the Anglican Church. She took on the role in Macao (a Portuguese territory on the coast of China) when priests could not travel there from Japanese-occupied territory during the Second World War. Once the war was over, she surrendered her priest's duties but resumed the practice of her priesthood in the 1980s. She is now regarded as one of the great Christian women of the twentieth century.

In 1994 the first women were ordained as priests in the Church of England. Many churches will not accept women priests, and there is a big debate about whether women should be bishops. The Roman Catholic Church ordains only men. It claims that this is not discrimination — women have a different role to play. Table 11.1 outlines some of the arguments in support of and against women priests.

**Table 11.1** Arguments for and against women priests

| Arguments against women priests | Arguments for women priests |
| --- | --- |
| Jesus chose only men as his disciples | Jesus did not choose women as his disciples because of the culture at the time |
| Some of Paul's teaching states that women are not to lead worship | In other passages Paul accepts women as having authority. In any case, society has changed since then |
| Having women priests has led to disunity in the Anglican Church. It would have been better to wait for a while | Sometimes a stand has to be made. Should Christians have waited until everyone agreed before they abolished slavery? |
| Men and women are essentially different | Women have a unique contribution to make |

# Martin Luther King Jr

Until the mid-twentieth century, black Americans were educated separately from whites and were not allowed access to the same facilities. Few had the right to vote, as this was dependent on literacy tests that required proof that you could read and write. As few black people were literate, these tests were a way of preventing them from voting. Thanks to the **civil rights movement** and **Black Power** groups, by 1965 black Americans were given the same status as white Americans. However, in practice there is still a deep racial divide. Although some black people such as Condoleezza Rice have been appointed to high positions in the US government, institutional racism is a major problem in some states.

Martin Luther King Jr was perhaps the most important leader of the civil rights movement. He was born in 1929, the son of a Baptist minister. During his college education, King was inspired by the teachings of Mahatma Gandhi. He became a Baptist minister in Montgomery, Alabama, and during his time there the civil rights movement was born. A black woman, Rosa Parks, was arrested in 1955 because she refused to give up her seat on a bus to a white man. This led to a bus boycott led by King, which continued despite intimidation until the law was changed.

### Key words

**Apartheid**
The policy of racial segregation and discrimination enforced by the white minority governments of South Africa

**Black Power**
A political movement among African Americans in the USA, which emphasised racial pride and promoted black interests

**Civil rights movement**
A movement that sought to gain justice for black people in the USA by non-violent means

**Ku Klux Klan (KKK)**
A white racist group in the USA

Over a period of 10 years, a series of non-violent protest marches and sit-ins took place. These continued despite the violent backlash from the **Ku Klux Klan (KKK)** and other racists. In a march on Washington in 1963, King gave his famous 'I have a dream' speech in which he stated his vision of an America where his children would be judged by their characters rather than the colour of their skin. In 1964 King was awarded the Nobel peace prize, and the following year black people were given the vote.

Throughout the campaign, King stuck to a policy of non-violence, even though he was harassed by whites and verbally abused by blacks who thought he was weak. He spoke about the evil of violence being overcome by the power of love. In 1968 he was assassinated.

## Nelson Mandela and Desmond Tutu

From 1948 until 1994, the South African government's policy of **apartheid** meant that the black majority had no rights at all. They were forcibly relocated to townships outside the cities and had little access to proper education, health services and leisure facilities. International pressure in the form of **sanctions** and isolation eventually forced change, and now all citizens have equal rights whatever their racial origins. Problems still exist, however, and the crime rate is high partly because black poverty has not been eradicated.

A slum for black South Africans during apartheid

During the terrible years of apartheid, two men came to different conclusions about the use of violence to change the system.

Nelson Mandela was brought up as a Methodist and trained as a lawyer. He joined the **African National Congress (ANC)** and tried in vain to achieve a change in the government's attitude by peaceful means. Eventually, he decided that violence was

### Key words

**African National Congress (ANC)**
A political party that was formed to increase the rights of black people in South Africa

**Sanctions**
Refusing to trade with a country or to supply what it needs

# Christian responsibility — Prejudice and discrimination

justified as the only way to destroy the evil system of apartheid, and in 1963 he was sentenced to life imprisonment for his activities. He was released in 1990 by President F. W. de Klerk, who realised that the system had to change if South Africa was to survive politically and economically. Apartheid was dismantled and, in 1994, Mandela became the first democratically elected president. He set about achieving his vision of South Africa as a 'rainbow people', created the **Truth and Reconciliation Commission** as a way of healing wounds, and ended his country's isolation from the rest of the world.

> **Key words**
>
> **Truth and Reconciliation Commission**
> A body that investigated the crimes committed by both black and white people during the apartheid era, in the hope of getting people to face up to what they had done and to seek and receive forgiveness from their victims

Desmond Tutu trained to become a priest. After his ordination he studied further at King's College in London, eventually returning to South Africa as a lecturer. He was made a bishop and then an archbishop, using his position of authority to campaign against apartheid. Despite experiencing harassment from the government, he never changed his views on non-violence. He refused to use the methods of his opponents, and in 1984 he was awarded the Nobel peace prize. After the overthrow of apartheid, he was put in charge of the Truth and Reconciliation Commission.

## Questions and activities

### Sample questions and answers

**1** Explain, giving examples, the difference between prejudice and discrimination. (3 marks)

*Answer*
Prejudice means having opinions about someone without good reason, e.g. someone might think all blonde women are unintelligent. Discrimination is when prejudice is acted upon, e.g. if someone refuses to give a blonde woman a job, even though she is the best qualified of all the applicants, because of the belief stated above.

#### Commentary
This question occurs quite frequently. It is essential that you know the difference between prejudice and discrimination.

## 2 Explain some of the reasons for prejudice. (4 marks)

The main cause of prejudice is ignorance. Some people do not understand why others behave in a certain way or dress in particular clothes. This sometimes makes them afraid. A man could hear a joke about women being bad drivers and, a short time afterwards, a woman drives into the back of his car. He thinks 'Typical woman' because he has been influenced by the views of others. That, together with his single bad experience, leads him to accept this stereotype of women.

### Commentary

This answer contains several reasons, with some discussion of them: ignorance, fear, influence of others, bad experience and stereotyping.

## 3 How might a Christian try to stop discrimination? (4 marks)

If the person is in a position of authority, he or she could use that position to influence others. For example, a priest could preach sermons against it. Even better, the pope could write an encyclical instructing all Roman Catholics not to discriminate against others. MPs can vote for laws that will prevent discrimination, and they can listen to and help anyone in their constituency who is a victim of it. Ordinary Christians can refuse to be part of any bullying or verbal abuse. They can make it clear that racist or sexist jokes are not funny. Above all, they can follow the example of Jesus and treat everyone with respect and kindness.

### Commentary

Because the question is worth 4 marks, both variety and development are needed. One way of achieving this is to approach the question from two different angles: an influential person and an ordinary religious believer. This enables good development to be made

## 4 Explain how one famous Christian has reflected Christian beliefs and teachings in his or her struggle against prejudice and discrimination. (4 marks)

Most of Martin Luther King Jr's adult life was devoted to the struggle for civil rights in the USA. Although he had a much better education than most black people of his day and could have led a comfortable life, he was willing to face persecution, harassment and imprisonment for what he believed in. He finally paid with his life, following Jesus's example

# Christian responsibility — Prejudice and discrimination

of self-sacrificial love. In his vision of a USA where all people would be treated the same regardless of their colour, he reflected the teaching of Paul that racial differences are unimportant to God and the belief that all humans are children of God. His refusal to use violence followed Jesus's teaching about turning the other cheek. Like Paul, he said that the way to overcome evil was to respond positively with good.

## Commentary

You are required to know how religious beliefs have influenced the life of one well-known Christian. The example given here is of Martin Luther King Jr. It is important to write about more than just the person's life. You need to refer to specific Christian teaching and show how that influenced his or her actions.

## Further questions

1 Give two types of discrimination. (2 marks)
2 Explain Christian beliefs and teachings about prejudice and discrimination. (4 marks)
3 'Christians are hypocrites. They say discrimination is wrong, but Christianity has been guilty of discrimination.' Do you agree? Give reasons for your answer, showing that you have thought about more than one point of view. (5 marks)

## Class activities and homework

### Types of prejudice

This section looks at three types of discrimination: racial, gender and disability. Your teacher will divide the class into small groups and give each group one of these types of discrimination to research in greater depth. Find out how the law deals with it, discuss why it is a problem and consider what measures could be taken to prevent it. Put together a short presentation to give to the rest of the class.

Find out about the work of a Christian organisation that campaigns against discrimination. Present your findings in a format that will be useful for your revision.

Find out more about and make notes on the life of Li Tim-Oi and the work of the Li Tim-Oi Foundation.

Effects of Christianity on Behaviour, Attitudes and Lifestyles

## Campaigning against discrimination

Watch a film or documentary about Martin Luther King Jr, Nelson Mandela, Desmond Tutu, the American civil rights movement or apartheid.

Talk to someone at the Citizens' Advice Bureau about the kind of advice and support that are available to victims of discrimination.

Explore www.britkid.org to find out about daily life from the perspectives of teenagers of different races and religions.

## Useful websites

www.anc.org.za   Click on *Site Index*, then on links listed under *ANC Sites* for information about Nelson Mandela.

www.bbc.co.uk   Type *Desmond Tutu* into the search engine for an audio interview and other web pages about him.

www.britkid.org

www.litim-oi.org

www.martinlutherking.8m.com

www.request.org.uk   Click on *main site*, then on *history* and look under '20th century and today' for information about the life of Martin Luther King.

www.theforgivenessproject.com

# Section 12

# World poverty

## The situation

Although only 25% of the world's population live in developed countries, they consume 80% of the world's resources. This suggests that greed and injustice play a part in the issue of global poverty. However, it is a complex problem.

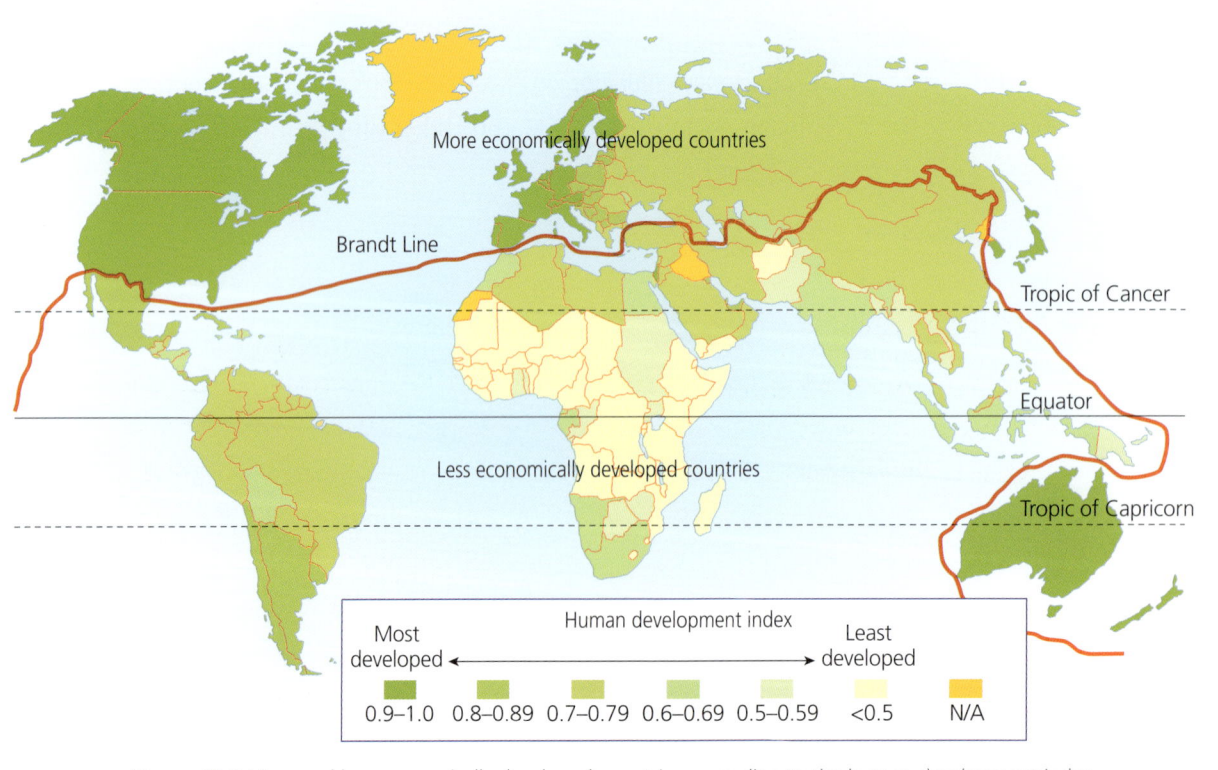

**Figure 12.1** More and less economically developed countries, according to the human development index

110  Effects of Christianity on Behaviour, Attitudes and Lifestyles

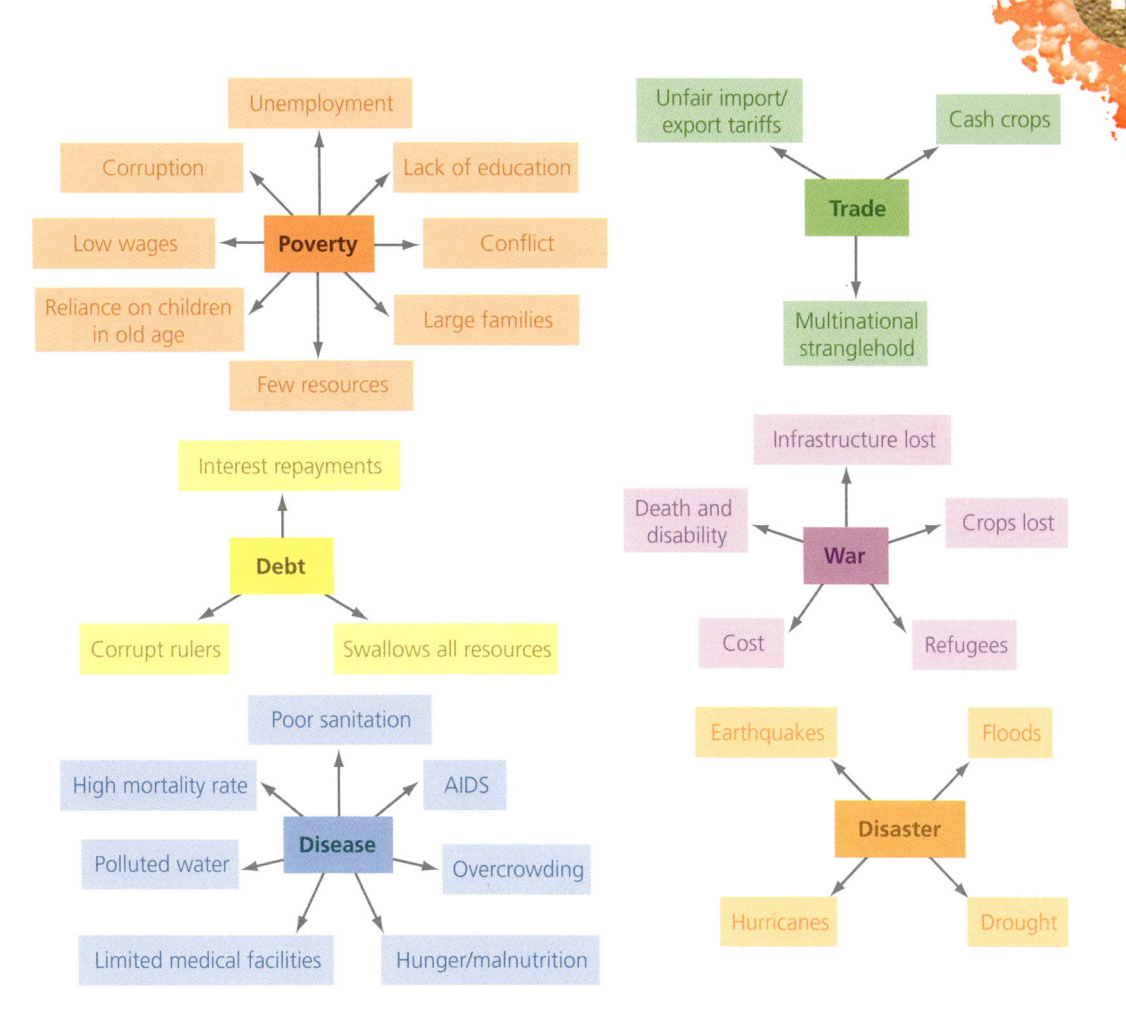

**Figure 12.2** Characteristics of less developed countries

## Natural disasters

Natural disasters such as droughts and hurricanes have always occurred, but climate change is likely to make them more frequent and severe. Their effects are made worse by other factors such as war, corrupt governments, debt and unfair trade.

## Disease

Disease is a huge problem in many less developed countries. One of the reasons for this is that pharmaceutical companies in the developed world focus on finding treatments for diseases that are most likely to affect their peoples, such as cancer and heart disease. Therefore, little money is spent on treatments for diseases like leprosy and malaria. Many diseases are caused by polluted water and poor

GCSE Religious Studies AQA (A) Option 2A

nutrition, but the countries facing these problems are too poor to deal with them by themselves. HIV/AIDS is a serious problem, but for many years the Western pharmaceutical companies would not sell drugs to treat this condition at a price that poor countries could afford.

## Education

Many children in less developed countries receive no education. Their families may need them to work to bring in money or to help on the land, or they may not be able to afford the school fees. Those who do receive education are often in large classes with little resources and equipment. Girls in particular may be denied an education.

## War

In a war-torn country, money that should be spent on supporting its citizens and building the economy is used to buy weapons and to repair roads and bridges. Those who work on the land may be either mercilessly slaughtered or forced into rebel armies, or they may flee to the towns to live on the streets or in shanty towns. In some cases, they escape into neighbouring countries, where they become refugees.

## Debt

Many less developed countries are crippled by debt. In the 1970s economic boom, Western governments and banks lent money to poorer countries that was often wasted on fighting wars and providing a luxurious lifestyle for their corrupt rulers. These countries have since experienced difficulties in repaying their debts. There have been major campaigns to pressurise world governments and financial institutions to cancel the debts. In Britain recently, there have been demonstrations and a great deal of pressure put on the government to improve the situation. Some of the debts were cancelled as a result.

## Unfair trade

Wealthy, developed countries hold most of the power when it comes to negotiating trade rules at meetings of the World Trade Organization (WTO). Governments of these countries want to support the best interests of multinational businesses which contribute to their economies. The **G8 summit** has been accused of promoting the interests of powerful Western countries at the expense of poorer countries.

Meanwhile, much of the farming in less developed countries is aimed at producing cash crops to pay off national debt rather than providing food for their citizens. In the 1980s, there was a dreadful famine in part of Ethiopia. However, unknown to many British people who saw harrowing scenes each night on television, in another part of Ethiopia red kidney beans were being grown for export to pay off some of the country's debt. Another problem for farmers in less developed countries is that cheap produce is imported from developed countries that want to get rid of their surplus, and local farmers cannot compete with such low prices.

### Key words

**G8 summit**
An annual meeting of leaders from the world's eight most powerful countries to discuss trade issues and world poverty

A Make Poverty History march during the G8 summit in Edinburgh, 2005

## Bad governments

Greed, corruption or incompetence on the part of its government can mean that any income a poor country receives does not benefit those in need. For example, instead of being spent on new hospitals and schools, the money is spent on building a grander palace for the president. Sometimes a nation's revenue is spent on a war against its own people, as in the Darfur region of Sudan. Governments may also avoid tackling problems such as HIV/AIDS.

## Population problems

The world's population has grown enormously over the past 50 years, and there are concerns that there will be insufficient resources for all. In less developed countries, families often have large numbers of children for several reasons:
- The lack of state benefits means that people are dependent on their children in old age.
- There is a high infant mortality rate, so parents may wish to have more children in case some of them die during childhood.
- Children are needed to help with farming and looking after animals.
- There is ignorance about or lack of access to contraception.
- There are religious or cultural objections to contraception.

# The response

Some governments are responding to the crisis, although more needs to be done. In the UK, there is a government department for international development that aims to promote sustainable development and eliminate world poverty. A small percentage of the national income is given to projects that focus on reducing poverty. At times of crisis, such as the 2004 Asian tsunami, larger sums are given for immediate relief.

Much of the response to world poverty comes from charities. There are many of these charities in Britain, some of which combine campaigning in the UK with involvement in particular projects in less developed countries. Some charities are religious organisations whereas others are secular.

Individuals can also get involved in a variety of ways:

- give money and items that are needed
- give time by working as a volunteer in a charity shop
- raise funds through participating in sponsored events
- become involved in campaigns, e.g. the Make Poverty History protest outside the G8 summit, or letter-writing campaigns to pressurise the government into action on poverty issues
- raise awareness by informing others
- gain skills that are needed in developing countries, and then work in one of these countries
- take time out of regular employment to work on a project in a developing country
- take part in voluntary work while travelling, e.g. during a gap year
- pray for people in need and those working with them

An organisation that has grown considerably in the past decade is the Fairtrade Foundation. Those involved in the **fair-trade** movement aim at getting a fair price for producers in poor countries. Many supermarkets now sell fair-trade produce such as coffee, tea and bananas. The price might be slightly higher than conventional items, but a much greater proportion of the money paid by the final consumer goes directly to the farmer or producer of the goods.

### Key words

**Fair trade**
A movement that ensures that the disadvantaged growers or producers in the developing world get a fair price for their goods

Fair trade is about better prices, decent working conditions, local sustainability and fair terms of trade for farmers and workers in the developing world

# Christian attitudes to world poverty

All Christians want to see an end to world poverty. They stress the importance of:
- justice — each person has the same rights to fair and equal treatment
- stewardship — humans are given the task of being responsible for and looking after those in need
- compassion — people should feel pity for others and want to do something to help
- following the example of Jesus, whose life and teaching showed his deep concern for the poor

Some Christians practise tithing, which means they give a tenth of their surplus income to religious and charitable causes. Others do not give a set amount but support particular charities. Many Christians give up what they regard as luxuries during Lent and donate the money they would have spent on them to the poor. Some churches organise weekly Lenten lunches. Those who come are given soup and a bread roll, and the money they would have spent on a meal is given to an organisation such as Christian Aid. One Christian denomination, the Salvation Army, is noted for its work with the poor both in the UK and around the world.

You need to know about the work of one of the following Christian organisations: Christian Aid, CAFOD, Trócaire or Tearfund. The ways in which they work vary, but they are all concerned with:
- long-term aid through projects intended to enable communities in less developed countries to become self-sufficient
- short-term or emergency relief
- campaigning to change attitudes in government and big businesses
- producing educational materials for schools and churches
- raising awareness through advertising and websites aimed at both adults and children
- fundraising

Christian Aid was set up to deal with the problem of refugees in Europe at the end of the Second World War, but since then has adapted to meet need on a global scale. It is interdenominational and is increasingly concerned with campaigning and highlighting justice issues as well as providing emergency and long-term aid. Christian Aid is part of the Make Poverty History campaign and the fair-trade movement. It helps whoever is in need, regardless of race, religion and culture.

Many Roman Catholics donate to CAFOD. This charity distributes money raised in England and Wales to various projects. It provides both emergency and long-term aid, working (like Christian Aid) through partners in the countries that need support. It is involved in campaigning and raising awareness through education, and is part of the Make Poverty History campaign and the fair-trade movement.

Trócaire was founded by the Roman Catholic Church in Ireland in 1973. It provides long-term and emergency aid, and raises awareness in communities and schools throughout Ireland. It works with partner organisations in less developed countries and is involved in a wide range of projects.

Tearfund is a Protestant organisation that works with many different churches throughout the world, providing long-term and emergency aid. It aims to meet the spiritual and physical needs of the poor. It evolved gradually in the 1960s and, like other aid agencies, also works to raise awareness in the UK.

Christian aid agencies and individual Christians are motivated to help others by biblical teaching. In the Old Testament, Jews are commanded to take care of the most vulnerable members of society, and a number of customs were established to help the poor. The New Testament states, 'If anyone has material possessions and sees his brother in need but has no pity on him, how can the love of God be in him?' (1 John 3:17). This passage reflects the teaching of Jesus that the two greatest commandments were to love God and your neighbour. In the parables of the rich fool, and the rich man and Lazarus, Jesus told his listeners to respond to those in need and to use their wealth to benefit others.

# Questions and activities

## Sample questions and answers

**1** Name two countries that are classed as less developed. (2 marks)

Tanzania and Bangladesh.

### Commentary

Two names are all that is required. This question is simply testing factual knowledge.

# Christian responsibility　　　World poverty

**2** Explain the difference between short-term (emergency) relief and long-term aid. **(2 marks)**

Short-term relief is aid that is given in response to a particular crisis, such as an earthquake. It is given for a relatively short period of time. Long-term aid refers to projects that are aimed at making individuals and communities self-sufficient and no longer dependent on charity.

## Commentary

As there are only 2 marks, a detailed answer is not necessary. You just need to show your understanding of the difference between the two types of aid.

**3** Explain two reasons for poverty in less developed countries. **(4 marks)**

One reason for poverty is debt. Many countries borrowed money a few decades ago from institutions in the developed world. When interest rates later soared, they were unable to repay the money. Another reason for poverty is war. Many people become refugees when they try to escape the fighting.

## Commentary

There are two marks for each reason, which means that a reason followed by a simple development is needed. Again, there is no need for a long answer.

**4** Explain how an individual Christian might help the poor. **(4 marks)**

Christians can help the poor in many ways. Those who are unable to give money because they cannot afford it, or those who cannot be actively involved because they are ill or disabled can pray for the poor and for the people trying to help them. Christians believe that God hears and answers their prayers. They can become involved in the work of an organisation like Christian Aid by organising fundraising activities in their communities and creating greater awareness of the needs of the poor and what Christian Aid does in countries such as Chad. Gap-year students could become volunteers, working on a secular or Christian project in the less developed world. Above all, parents can ensure

Effects of Christianity on Behaviour, Attitudes and Lifestyles

that their children grow up to desire justice for the poor and to see themselves as stewards rather than owners of their wealth, with a duty to use it wisely for the good of all humanity.

## Commentary

This question requires detailed comment on several ways in which the poor might be helped. In view of the word 'Christian' in the question, it is important that there is some religious content in the answer.

## Further questions

1 Explain why Christians think they should help the poor. (5 marks)
2 Describe the work of one Christian voluntary agency. (5 marks)
3 'Countries are only poor because they have bad governments. They should sort out their problems themselves.' Do you agree? Give reasons for your answer, showing that you have thought about more than one point of view. Refer to Christian teaching in your answer. (5 marks)

## Class activities and homework

### Aid agencies

Find out more about the Christian voluntary agencies you are studying. Create an A4-size poster on each, giving information about the organisation in a way that will be eye-catching and will encourage people to think about becoming involved.

Your teacher will divide the class into groups and give each group an aid project to research. Prepare a short talk for the rest of the class on that project.

Using the websites suggested below, find out more about recent and current campaigns to abolish debt and unfair trade.

### Fair trade

Play one of the fair-trade games produced by Christian Aid or CAFOD. Discuss in groups or as a whole class how you felt as you played and what you have learned.

GCSE Religious Studies AQA (A) Option 2A

## Christian responsibility — World poverty

**Homework:** Research and make bullet point notes on the aims and activities of Traidcraft.

## Useful websites

www.cafod.org.uk

www.christian-aid.org.uk

www.fairtrade.org.uk

www.jubileedebtcampaign.org.uk

www.karuna.org

www.makepovertyhistory.org

www.request.org.uk  Click on *main site*, then on *action* for information on Christian aid agencies; click on *issues* for views on wealth and poverty.

www.tearfund.org

www.traidcraft.co.uk

# Section 13

# Biblical passages

## The centurion's servant: Luke 7:1–10

A centurion was a Roman army officer and most Jews would have hated him because he was a **Gentile** and a member of the occupying army. The Jews of Capernaum were prepared to tolerate him, however, because he was interested in their faith and had financed the building of the synagogue. When his servant fell ill, they were willing to go to Jesus on his behalf to ask for his help. Jesus immediately set off for the centurion's house, but while he was on the way the centurion sent some friends to give Jesus a message. They said the centurion thought he did not deserve to have Jesus in his house or to meet him in person, and if Jesus would simply say the word he knew the servant would be healed. He was used to giving and receiving orders and recognised Jesus's authority in the sphere of healing. Jesus was amazed by this and said he had never found such faith even among Jews. When the messengers returned to the house, they found the servant well again.

> **Key word**
> **Gentile**
> Non-Jew

This is an important story because it shows Jesus's attitude to Gentiles. By being prepared to go to the centurion's house, he was showing his acceptance of him as an equal. According to Jewish law, entering a Gentile's house made a Jew unclean. Jesus also praised the centurion's faith, saying it was greater than that of Jews. This is a warning against racial prejudice and discrimination.

**Christian responsibility**     **Biblical passages**

# The good Samaritan: Luke 10:25–37

An expert in Jewish law asked Jesus how to gain eternal life. Jesus asked him what the Scriptures said, and he replied that they taught wholehearted love of God and of one's neighbour. Jesus told him he was right, but the man went on to ask, 'And who is my neighbour?' In response, Jesus told the parable of the good Samaritan.

Painting of the good Samaritan story by van Gogh

Effects of Christianity on Behaviour, Attitudes and Lifestyles

A Jew was walking along the dangerous road between Jerusalem and Jericho when he was mugged and left to die. A rabbi and a Levite (temple official) came by, one after the other. Both crossed over to the other side of the road when they saw the man. Eventually, a Samaritan passed by. Jews and Samaritans were bitter enemies, but the Samaritan stopped, bandaged up the man, put him on his donkey and took him to an inn. The Samaritan paid the innkeeper for the man's care, telling him that if any more money was needed he would pay on his return. At this point, Jesus asked his questioner who had been the neighbour to the mugged man. 'The one who had mercy on him,' the man replied. Jesus simply said, 'Go and do likewise.'

In this parable not only does the Samaritan help his enemy, he is also the enemy of those listening. Jesus might have got the point across less controversially if the story had been about a Jew who helped a Samaritan. Jesus was saying that being a neighbour means helping anyone in need — and showing a willingness to accept help — regardless of culture, religious belief or race.

# Peter and Cornelius: Acts 11:1–18

This is a story relating to the development of the early Church. Peter, one of Jesus's Apostles and a leading figure in the Christian community, was called to account by other leading Christians for going into a Gentile's home and eating there. The first Christians were all Jewish and kept to Jewish laws, which prohibited what Peter had done. Peter explained what had happened. While he was in Joppa, he had a vision in which a sheet was lowered from the sky. Inside were all kinds of creatures, clean and unclean. When a voice from heaven told him to kill and eat, he refused on the grounds that he had never eaten anything that was unclean. The voice replied, 'Do not call anything impure that God has made clean.' This happened three times and then the vision ended. At that moment some messengers arrived, asking Peter to go with them to go to a house in Caesarea. Guided by the Spirit to do so, he went and was told by Cornelius (who was a Roman centurion and therefore a Gentile) that he had experienced a vision telling him to send for Peter. As Peter began to speak, Cornelius and the rest of the household were filled with the Spirit, speaking in tongues just as the 12 Apostles had done at the feast of Pentecost. Peter concluded his defence by saying, 'So if God gave them the same gift as he gave us,

**Christian responsibility** | **Biblical passages**

who believed in the Lord Jesus Christ, who was I to think that I could oppose God?' Peter's critics accepted what he said, recognising that God's salvation was on offer to Gentiles, too.

This story marked an important stage in the development of the Church, when it became clear that Gentiles could be accepted without having to follow Jewish law. As God does not make racial distinctions, neither should Christians.

## All one in Christ: Galatians 3:28

In one of his letters to the Galatians, Paul stated, 'There is neither Jew nor Greek, slave nor free, male nor female, for you are all one in Christ Jesus.' Paul's message here is that for Christians there should be no racial, social or gender distinctions — all are of equal significance in God's eyes.

## The sheep and the goats: Matthew 25:31–46

A shepherd on the hills above Bethlehem. Palestinian farmers have mixed flocks, but at nightfall they separate the sheep from the goats

This passage contains a parable that Jesus told about Judgement Day. He pictured all the nations of the world being gathered before him. He would divide everyone into two groups — one on the left and one on the right — just as a shepherd at Jesus's time would separate the sheep from the goats. He would welcome those on his right to eternal joy with God:

> For I was hungry and you gave me something to eat, I was thirsty and you gave me something to drink, I was a stranger and you invited me in, I needed clothes and you clothed me, I was sick and you looked after me, I was in prison and you came to visit me.

Effects of Christianity on Behaviour, Attitudes and Lifestyles

The people listening were amazed, and asked Jesus when they had seen him hungry and when they had fulfilled his needs. Jesus replied, 'I tell you the truth, whatever you did for one of the least of these brothers of mine, you did for me.' Then Jesus stated that those on his left were not to enjoy God's presence as they had failed to act like those on his right. They asked when they had failed to do so and he said that whenever they failed to help others, they failed him.

Jesus was teaching that what matters is how people treat one another and how they respond to others in need.

# The rich fool: Luke 12:13–21

A man in the crowd asked Jesus to make his brother share an inheritance with him. Jesus declined to intervene and went on to warn the crowd against greed, saying that material possessions were not what really counted. Jesus then told a parable about a farmer who had a bumper harvest. He wanted to make sure that when he sold his crops the price would be high, so he built new barns in which to store them. He congratulated himself on the fact that he had no need to work for many years but could eat, drink and enjoy himself. God told the man that he was a fool, for that night he would die and everything he had hoarded would be of no use to him.

This parable teaches us that material wealth is not everything and Christians should share what they have with those in need.

# The rich man and Lazarus: Luke 16:19–31

In this parable Jesus spoke of a rich man living in luxury, who did not help a beggar called Lazarus who lay hungry and diseased at his gate. Both men eventually died: Lazarus went to heaven and the rich man went to hell. The rich man asked Abraham to send Lazarus down with some water to cool his tongue, but Abraham said this was not possible and that they were both receiving what they deserved for their previous lives. The rich man then asked Abraham to send Lazarus back to earth to warn his brothers of their fate unless they changed their ways. Abraham refused, saying that they had the teachings of the Jewish Scriptures and that if they did not heed those then nothing could change them.

**Christian responsibility**     **Biblical passages**

This story is a warning that greed and indifference to the plight of the poor might have eternal consequences. There is no excuse for Christians not to respond to those in need, for they have the Bible, which teaches the need for compassion.

## Barnabas and the early Church: Acts 4:32–37

This short passage tells how, in the early days of the Christian Church, believers shared what they had with those who were poor so that no one was in need. The custom was to sell any possessions they did not need and bring the money to the Apostles, who shared it out among the poor. There was a Christian called Barnabas who came from Cyprus, where he had a field. He sold the field and handed over the proceeds of the sale to the Apostles.

This story encourages Christians to share what they have with those in need.

# Exam technique

When answering questions, always note:
- the command word
- the number of marks available

## Command words

These tell you the kind of answer that is needed:
- *Describe* means that you need to give information.
- *Give* usually requires you to state basic pieces of information or reasons for something.
- *Explain* requires some comment on facts or beliefs, e.g. 'Explain how religious believers might help the poor.' Do not just give a list, but discuss the points you make. Use examples to help you do this.
- *Do you agree? Give reasons for your answer, showing that you have thought about more than one point of view. Refer to Christian teaching in your answer.* This requires you to argue a case for two different (though not necessarily opposing) points of view and explain why you agree with one of them. If you're not sure where you stand on an issue, don't be afraid to say so, but explain why you either disagree with both arguments or find it hard to decide. To move beyond Level 3 (3 marks out of 5) you have to give two points of view, and you also have to include Christian argument. You don't have to be a Christian yourself or agree with the viewpoint, but you need to show that you can see how religious beliefs might affect someone's views on the issue.

## Marks available

These are given at the end of each part of a question and give you some idea of the type of answer required, and how much to write.
- *Do you agree? Give…* questions are always marked out of 5. You need to write two (or more) paragraphs and a conclusion in which it is clear what your view is.
- *Give* questions attract 3 marks at the most, and ask for one, two or three pieces of information, depending on the number of marks. Don't write at length.
- Questions with 1 mark require a word, phrase or very short sentence.

# Exam technique

- Where *describe*, *how*, *why* or *explain* are used, look at the number of marks available. The more marks, the more you need to write, and the more likely it is that more than a list is required.

## Timing

This is crucial. If you do not have time to answer one or more of the questions, you may end up a grade lower. If you only have time for one of the structured essays, you will lose 20 marks, and even if all your other answers are outstanding, you cannot be awarded more than 60 marks out of a total of 80.

- Keep an eye on the clock.
- Where one-word answers are required, write one word.
- If you are unable to answer a question, don't dither. Go on to the next and come back to it later.
- If you make a mistake, just cross it out. If you've written a lot, a quick diagonal line through is enough — don't neatly cross out each word or line.

## Quality of written communication

There are up to 3 marks available for the quality of your writing, marks that are worth having as they could improve your grade. They are given for your ability:

- to spell and use punctuation
- to write legibly
- to use grammar correctly, so that your meaning is clear

# Glossary

## A

**Abortion** The deliberate termination of a pregnancy

**Absolute morality** A type of morality that has fixed and unchanging rules

**Active euthanasia** Deliberately ending the life of someone who is seriously ill

**Adultery** A sexual relationship between two people, at least one of whom is married to someone else

**African National Congress (ANC)** A political party that was formed to increase the rights of black people in South Africa

**Annulment** The declaration that a valid marriage never existed

**Apartheid** The policy of racial segregation and discrimination enforced by the white minority governments of South Africa

**Assisi Declarations** Statements relating to the environment made by leaders of world religions

**Autonomy** The right to make decisions for yourself

## B

**Black Power** A political movement among African Americans in the USA, which emphasised racial pride and promoted black interests

**British National Party (BNP)** A far-right political party in the UK

## C

**Campaign for Nuclear Disarmament (CND)** An organisation that supports unilateral disarmament

**Capital punishment** The death penalty

**Casual sex** Sex without commitment

**Catechism of the Catholic Church** A book containing the official teaching of the Roman Catholic Church on all matters of faith and practice

**Celibacy** Not having a sexual relationship within or outside marriage, often as a result of a religious promise

**Chastity** Having moral standards and restraint with regard to sexual relations

**Christian denominations** The different Christian traditions, e.g. Anglican, Roman Catholic

**Civil partnership ceremonies** Non-religious ceremonies that allow gay couples to legally register their partnerships

# Glossary

**Civil rights movement** A movement that sought to gain justice for black people in the USA by non-violent means

**Cohabitation** A couple living together and enjoying a sexual relationship without being married

**Contraception** A range of methods that may be used to prevent pregnancy

**Crime** An offence committed against the law of the land

# D

**Discrimination** Putting prejudice into action

# E

**Ensoulment** The point at which the foetus receives its soul from God, and therefore becomes a person

**Equality** The idea that everyone is of equal importance and value, and should be treated as such

**Eucharist** One of the Christian sacraments, a service at which Christians eat bread and drink wine in remembrance of Jesus's death

**Euthanasia** The deliberate termination of a life in order to end someone's suffering

**Extra-marital sex** A sexual relationship between two people who are not married to each other. They may be single or married to someone else

# F

**Fair trade** A movement that ensures that disadvantaged growers or producers in the developing world get a fair price for their goods

**Foetal rights** The rights of the unborn child

**Forgiveness** Pardoning someone for what they have done and not holding it against them

**Fundamentalist Christian** Someone who believes that the Bible was inspired directly by God and contains no errors. Its teachings are always relevant

# G

**G8 summit** An annual meeting of leaders from the world's eight most powerful countries to discuss trade issues and world poverty

**Gentile** Non-Jew

# H

**Homosexuality** Being attracted to people of the same sex

**Hospice** A place that provides care for terminally ill patients

# I

**Institutional racism** Racial prejudice and discrimination that are said to be at the heart of some organisations

**Intifada** Palestinian uprising against Israel's occupation of their land

**Involuntary euthanasia** Ending someone's life without his or her consent

# J

**Justice** Treating everyone fairly and equally

**'Just' war theory** Set of conditions to be met if war is to be justified

# K

**Ku Klux Klan (KKK)** A white racist group in the USA

**Kyoto Treaty** An international agreement to cut back on carbon emissions and deal with environmental problems. The USA is the biggest polluter but has refused to commit itself

# L

**Liberal Christian** Someone who believes that God guided the writers of the Bible, but that there are mistakes and some of its teachings are out of date

**Living wills** These tell medical staff about how patients wish to be treated at the end of their lives, should they be unable to communicate their wishes

# M

**Macmillan nurse** A nurse who is specially trained in palliative care for cancer patients

**Martyr** Someone who dies for his or her faith

**Maternal rights** The rights of the mother

**Multilateral disarmament** Nations disposing of nuclear weapons by mutual agreement

# N

**Non-voluntary euthanasia** Ending the life of a sick person who is incapable of requesting death

**Nuptial Mass** A service of Holy Communion held as part of the marriage ceremony

# O

**Original sin** A tendency to sin that humans are born with

# Glossary

# P

**Pacifist** Someone who is opposed to violence

**Palliative care** Specialised care that relieves pain and distress

**Passive euthanasia** Letting a person die without medical intervention

**Peace** Being able to live without fear of harm and to fulfil your potential

**Permanent vegetative state (PVS)** An irreversible condition caused by the destruction of the neo-cortical area of the brain

**Prejudice** An irrational opinion about an individual or group

**Pre-marital sex** Sexual intercourse prior to marriage

**Pro-choice** Supporting the right of women to decide for themselves whether or not to have an abortion

**Procreative sex** Sex which has the possibility of conception

**Pro-life** The anti-abortion view that the foetus has absolute right to life

# Q

**Quality of life** Whether or not a person will have a life that is worthwhile and of value

# R

**Reconciliation** One of the Christian sacraments. It involves confessing your sins to a priest and the priest declaring God's forgiveness

**Relative morality** A type of morality which takes the situation and circumstances into account

**Responsibility** The duties that humans have because of the power they exercise

# S

**Sacrament** An outward action or ceremony that gives a spiritual blessing

**Sacramental covenant** A sacred contract involving promises. It is a binding agreement in which God acts as witness

**Sanctions** Refusing to trade with a country and to supply what it needs

**Sanctity of life** The idea that life is holy and precious

**Scapegoating** Blaming an innocent individual or group for something that is wrong

**Secular** Not religious

**Sin** A religious offence

**Stereotyping** Creating an oversimplified image of an individual or group, usually by assuming that all members of the group are the same

**Stewardship** Humans do not own the world but should look after it responsibly on behalf of God

**St Francis of Assisi** Patron saint of animals and a role model for environmental concern

**Suffragette movement** A reform movement in the early twentieth century that aimed to secure the right for women to vote

# T

**Trimester** A period of 3 months. Pregnancy may be divided into three trimesters

**Truth and Reconciliation Commission** A body that investigated the crimes committed by both black and white people in South Africa during the apartheid era, in the hope of getting people to face up to what they had done and to seek and receive forgiveness from their victims

# U

**Unilateral disarmament** A nation disposing of its nuclear weapons regardless of what other countries do

**Unitive sex** The idea that sexual intercourse makes a couple one

# V

**Viability** The point in development at which a baby could be born with some chance of independent survival

**Voluntary euthanasia** Ending a person's life at his or her request

# Useful websites

You may find these websites useful throughout your course. Websites that relate to particular topics have been listed at the end of the appropriate sections.

http://news.bbc.co.uk

www.bbc.co.uk

www.channel4.com

For these sites, use the search engine to direct you to the information that you need.

www.bbc.co.uk/schools/gcsebitesize/re

A revision site.

http://re-xs.ucsm.ac.uk

This site covers world religions, ethical issues and also directs you to other websites.

www.request.org.uk

This site gives information on Christian beliefs, practices and responses to issues. It also gives information on famous Christians.

# Index

Page numbers in **bold** type indicate the main definition of each key word and glossary term.

## A

abortion  *23–34*
   arguments for and against  *26–27*
   Biblical passages  *54*
   central issues  *27–29*
   definition  **23**, *129*
   laws in the UK  *23–26*
   questions and activities  *31–34*
   sexual relationships  *9*
   sources of morality  *4*
absolute morality  *1*, **4–5**, *129*
active euthanasia  *37*, *39*, *129*
adultery
   Biblical passages  *54*, *94*
   crime and punishment  *71*
   definition  **9**, *129*
   sex, marriage and divorce  *9*, *11*, *17*
African National Congress (ANC)  *105*, *129*
Al Qaeda  *79*
ANC *see* African National Congress
Anglican Church
   abortion  *31*
   crime and punishment  *71*
   prejudice and discrimination  *102*, *103*
   sex, marriage and divorce  *13*, *15*, *17*, *18–19*
   sources of morality  *4*
   war and peace  *82*
annulment  *17*, **18**, *129*
anti-social behaviour orders (ASBOs)  *66*
apartheid  *59*, *104*, *105*, *106*, *129*
ASBOs *see* anti-social behaviour orders
Asian tsunami  *114*
Assisi Declarations  *48*, *129*
atomic weapons  *78*
autonomy  *27*, *38*, **39**, *129*

## B

Benedict XVI, Pope  *2*, *3*
Bible
   abortion  *29*
   Christian moral decision-making  *2*, *4*, *5*
   Christian responsibility  *121–26*
   decisions on life and living  *52–56*
   environment  *47*
   justice and reconciliation  *88–94*
   peace  *60*
   sex, marriage and divorce  *9*, *10*, *11*, *12*, *15*, *18*
biological weapons  *78*
Black Power  *104*, *129*
BNP *see* British National Party
Bonhoeffer, Dietrich  *68*, *82*, *86*
British National Party (BNP)  *97*, *129*
Burma  *83*

## C

CAFOD (Catholic Agency for Overseas Development)  *48*, *116*, *117*
Campaign for Nuclear Disarmament (CND)  *78*, *81*, *83*, *129*
capital punishment
   crime and punishment  *67–68*, *71*, *73*
   definition  **67**, *129*
   justice and reconciliation  *93*, *94*
casual sex  **9**, *11*, *129*
Catechism of the Catholic Church
   abortion  *29*, *30*
   crime and punishment  *71*
   definition  **4**, *129*
   prejudice and discrimination  *101*
   war and peace  *82*
Catherine of Siena  *103*

# Index

Catholics *see* Roman Catholics
celibacy  *10, 129*
charities  *114, 115, 116, 117*
**Charles, Prince of Wales**  *19*
chastity  *10, 129*
chemical weapons  *78*
**Christian Aid**  *48, 116*
Christian attitudes
   abortion  *29-31*
   Christian moral decision-making  *1-6*
   crime and punishment  *68-71*
   divorce and remarriage  *17-19*
   environment  *47-48*
   euthanasia  *39*
   marriage  *12-15*
   prejudice and discrimination  *101-03*
   sexual relationships  *9-11*
   war and peace  *81-83*
   world poverty  *116-17*
Christian denominations  *2, 129*
**Christian Ecology Link**  *48*
**Christian Peacemaker Teams**  *83*
Christian responsibility
   Biblical passages  *121-26*
   prejudice and discrimination  *96-109*
   world poverty  *110-20*
*The Church and the Bomb*  *82*
**Church of England General Synod**  *47, 82*
   *see also* Anglican Church
civil marriage ceremony  *19*
civil partnership ceremonies  *8, 129*
civil rights movement  *104, 130*
**CND** *see* Campaign for Nuclear Disarmament
cohabitation  *9, 130*
command words  *127*
**Commission for Racial Equality (CRE)**  *98*
**Community of the Cross of Nails (CCN)**  *59*
community service  *65*
**Confessing Church**  *82*
conscience  *4*
contraception  *9, 15, 27, 114, 130*
conventional weapons  *77-78*

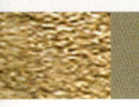

**Coventry Cathedral**  *59, 60*
**Cox, Dr Nigel**  *35*
crime and punishment  *62-74*
   aims of punishment  *64*
   capital punishment  *67-68*
   Christian attitudes  *68-71*
   crime and sin  *62*
   definition of crime  *62, 130*
   forms of punishment  *64-66*
   justice  *58*
   questions and answers  *71-74*
   why do people commit crime?  *63*
curfews  *65*

# D

**Darfur**  *114*
death penalty *see* capital punishment
debt  *111, 112, 113*
decisions on life and living
   abortion  *23-34*
   Biblical passages  *52-56*
   environment  *43-51*
   euthanasia  *35-42*
   sex, marriage and divorce  *8-22*
**de Klerk, President F. W.**  *106*
**Diana, Princess of Wales**  *77*
Didache  *30*
**Dignity in Dying organisation**  *37*
disability
   abortion  *24-27, 30, 31, 32-33*
   prejudice and discrimination  *100-101*
**Disability Discrimination Act 1995**  *101*
discrimination
   causes of prejudice and discrimination  *96-97*
   Christian attitudes  *101-03*
   definition  *96, 130*
   Desmond Tutu  *104-06*
   disability discrimination  *100-101*
   discrimination and the law  *97*
   gender discrimination  *99-100*
   Martin Luther King Jr  *103-04*

   Nelson Mandela  *104–06*
   racial discrimination  *97–98*
divorce  *16–19, 54*
droughts  *43, 45, 111*

# E

electronic tagging  *65*
Enniskillen bombing  *60*
ensoulment  *28, 130*
environment  *43–51*
   Biblical passages  *54*
   environmental problems  *43–45*
   questions and answers  *48–51*
   what can be done?  *45–46*
equality  *101, 102, 130*
Equal Opportunities Commission  *100*
Equal Pay Act 1970  *100*
Ethiopia  *113*
Eucharist  *18, 130*
euthanasia  *35–42*
   arguments for and against  *38*
   Biblical passages  *54*
   definition  *35, 130*
   questions and answers  *40–42*
   sources of morality  *4*
   types  *36–37*
exam technique  *127–28*
extra-marital sex  *9, 55, 130*

# F

fair trade  *115, 116, 117, 130*
Fairtrade Foundation  *115*
flooding  *44, 45*
foetal rights  *24, 25, 27, 130*
forgiveness
   crime and punishment  *70*
   definition  *60, 130*
   justice and reconciliation  *60–61, 88–89, 90, 92*
   war and peace  *82*
Friends of the Earth  *46*

fundamentalist Christians  *2, 5, 13, 56, 130*

# G

Gandhi, Mahatma  *104*
gay people *see* homosexuality
G8 summit  *112, 113, 115, 130*
gender discrimination  *99–100, 102–03*
General Synod  *47, 82*
genetics  *63*
Geneva Conventions  *77, 78*
Gentiles  *121, 123, 124, 130*
global warming  *43, 45*
good Samaritan  *122–23*
greenhouse gases  *45*
Green Party  *46*
Greenpeace  *46*

# H

Hildegard of Bingen  *103*
Hiroshima  *78*
HIV/AIDS (human immunodeficiency virus/acquired immune deficiency syndrome)  *112, 114*
homosexuality  *8, 130*
hospices  *37, 38, 130*
Human Genome Project  *63*

# I

imprisonment  *64–65, 70, 72, 73*
institutional racism  *98, 104, 131*
intifada  *79, 131*
involuntary euthanasia  *36, 38, 131*
IRA (Irish Republican Army)  *60–61*
Iraq war  *83*

# J

Jepson, Rev Joanna  *26, 33*
Jesus Christ
   Christian responsibility  *122–23, 124, 125*
   crime and punishment  *68, 70, 71*

# Index

environment  *48*
justice and reconciliation  *59, 61, 88–90, 91–93*
prejudice and discrimination  *101*
sex, marriage and divorce  *11, 12, 17, 18, 19, 54*
war and peace  *82*
world poverty  *117*
John XXIII, Pope  *82*
Julian of Norwich, Mother  *103*
justice and reconciliation
Biblical passages  *88–94*
crime and punishment  *62–74*
definition of justice  *58, 131*
overview  *58–61*
prejudice and discrimination  *101*
questions and answers  *61*
war and peace  *75–87*
world poverty  *116*
'just' war theory  *58, 80, 82, 131*

# K

Kember, Norman  *83*
Kent, Bruce  *81*
KKK *see* Ku Klux Klan
Kolbe, Maximilian  *3*
Ku Klux Klan (KKK)  *104, 131*
Kyoto Treaty  *45, 131*

# L

landmines  *77*
law  *23–26, 68, 97, 98, 100, 101*
Lebanon  *77*
Lent  *116*
liberal Christians  *2, 5, 131*
life (beginning of)  *28*
Li Tim-Oi  *3, 103*
living wills  *37, 38, 131*
Lord's Prayer  *70*
Lucas, Matt  *8*
Luther King Jr, Martin  *3, 68, 103–04*

# M

Macmillan nurses  *38, 131*
Make Poverty History  *113, 115, 116, 117*
Mandela, Nelson  *3, 105–06*
marriage  *11–16*
Biblical passages  *55–56*
Christian attitudes  *12–15*
divorce, annulment and remarriage  *17, 18*
overview  *11–12*
questions and answers  *19–22*
sexual relationships  *10, 11*
why marriages fail  *15–16*
martyrs  *82, 131*
maternal rights  *24, 26, 27, 131*
Mawdsley, James  *83*
Methodists  *31*
Moor, Dr David  *35*
morality  *1–6*
overview  *1*
questions and activities  *4–6*
sources  *2–4*
multilateral disarmament  *78, 82, 131*

# N

Nagasaki  *78*
natural disasters  *111*
non-voluntary euthanasia  *36, 38, 131*
nuclear weapons  *4, 78, 82, 83*
Nuptial Mass  *15, 131*

# O

original sin  *68, 131*
ozone layer  *45*

# P

pacifism  *58, 60, 80, 81, 132*
Palestine  *79*
palliative care  *38, 132*
Parks, Rosa  *104*

parole  65
passive euthanasia  37, 39, 132
Paul
   Christian responsibility  124
   justice and reconciliation  94
   prejudice and discrimination  102
   sex, marriage and divorce  10, 13, 17, 54-55
   war and peace  82
Pax Christi  81
peace  60, 61, 132
peace-keeping forces  77
permanent vegetative state (PVS)  39, 132
Playfoot, Lydia  11
pollution  44, 46, 47, 111
popes  2, 3, 4, 82
positive discrimination  96
poverty  110-20
   Christian attitudes  116-17
   questions and answers  117-20
   sources of morality  4
prejudice and discrimination  96-109
   causes  96-97
   Christian attitudes  101-03
   definition of prejudice  96, 132
   Desmond Tutu  104-06
   disability discrimination  100-101
   discrimination and the law  97
   gender discrimination  99-100
   Martin Luther King Jr  103-04
   Nelson Mandela  104-06
   questions and answers  106-09
   racial discrimination  97-98
pre-marital sex  9, 132
Pretty, Diane  36
prison  64-65, 70, 72, 73
probation  65
pro-choice  27, 132
procreative sex  15, 132
pro-life  27, 37, 132
Pro-Life Alliance  37
protest  83

punishment
   aims  64
   capital punishment  67-68
   Christian attitudes  69-71
   forms  64-66
   justice and reconciliation  58, 59, 60-61
PVS *see* permanent vegetative state

# Q

Quakers  71, 81
quality of life  29, 37, 38, 39, 132

# R

Race Relations Act (1976)  98
racial discrimination  97-98, 103-05
rainforests  45
rape  26, 27, 30, 31
reason (in moral decisions)  4
reconciliation  59-60, 82, 88, 89
Reconciliation (sacrament)  18, 132
recycling  45
relative morality  1, 4-5, 132
religious leaders  2-3
Religious Society of Friends (Quakers)  71, 81
remarriage  16, 17, 18, 19, 54
responsibility  47, 53, 132
Rice, Condoleezza  104
Roman Catholics
   abortion  29-31
   crime and punishment  71
   euthanasia  39
   prejudice and discrimination  103
   sex, marriage and divorce  10, 13, 15, 17-18
   sources of morality  2, 4
   world poverty  117
Romero, Oscar  3, 68, 69

# S

sacrament  17, 18, 132
sacramental covenant  12, 132

# Index

Salvation Army  *116*
sanctions  *105, 132*
sanctity of life  *29, 47, 53, 55, 132*
scapegoating  *97, 132*
secular groups  *15, 132*
Sentamu, John  *102*
Sex Discrimination Act 1975  *100*
sex, marriage and divorce  *8–22*
   divorce, annulment and remarriage  *16–19*
   marriage  *11–16*
   questions and answers  *19–22*
   sexual relationships  *8–11, 12, 15, 54–55*
Siamese twins  *4–5*
'Silver Ring Thing' movement  *10, 22*
sin  *62, 132*
Sosa, Lucia  *30*
stereotyping  *97, 132*
stewardship  *47, 53, 116, 133*
St Francis of Assisi  *48, 133*
Suffragette movement  *99, 133*
suicide bombers  *79*

## T

Tearfund  *48, 116, 117*
teenage sexuality  *9, 10*
Ten Commandments  *53–54*
Teresa of Calcutta, Mother  *3*
terrorism  *78, 79*
tithing  *116*
trade  *111, 112–13, 115–17*
trimester  *25, 133*
Trócaire  *116, 117*
'True Love Waits'  *10, 12, 22*
Truth and Reconciliation Commission  *59, 106, 133*
tsunami  *114*

Tutu, Desmond  *3, 68, 106*

## U

unfair trade  *111, 112–13*
unilateral disarmament  *78, 133*
United Nations (UN)  *77, 80*
unitive sex  *15, 133*

## V

Vatican Declaration on Euthanasia  *4, 39*
viability  *23, 133*
voluntary euthanasia  *36, 37, 38, 133*

## W

war and peace  *75–87*
   causes of war  *75*
   consequences of war  *75–77*
   justice  *58*
   'just' war theory  *80*
   pacifism  *80–81*
   protest  *83*
   questions and answers  *83–87*
   reconciliation  *60*
   terrorism  *79*
   types of weapons and warfare  *77–78*
   world poverty  *111, 112*
weapons  *77–78*
wedding ceremony  *13–15*
Wilson, Gordon  *60*
women priests  *103*
world poverty  *110–20*
   Christian attitudes  *116–17*
   questions and answers  *117–20*
   sources of morality  *4*
World Trade Organization (WTO)  *112*